The Greatest Gifts Our Children Give to Us

THE SURPRISING WISDOM OF KIDS

by Steven W. Vannoy

A Fireside Book
Simon & Schuster
New York

FIRESIDE
Rockefeller Center
1230 Avenue of the Americas
New York, NY 10020

FIRESIDE and colophon are registered trademarks
of Simon & Schuster Inc.

Designed by Jennifer Ann Daddio

Manufactured in the United States of America

1   3   5   7   9   10   8   6   4   2

Library of Congress Cataloging-in-Publication Data
Vannoy, Steven W.
The greatest gifts our children give to us :
the surprising wisdom of kids / by Steven W. Vannoy.
p.   cm.
1. Parent and child—Anecdotes.
2. Children and adults—Anecdotes
3. Parents—Conduct of life.   I. Title.
HQ755.85.V35   1997
649'.1—dc21   97-21625
CIP
ISBN 0-684-82397-7

Acknowledgments

To capture the exquisite gifts of children took an equally exquisite team. I wish to thank the following people for their dedication, energy, expertise, and commitment:

Allison St. Claire, Jody Rein, Fred Hills, Burton Beals, Hilary Black, Donna Carter, Pandora Reagan, Denise Pushnik, Margo Yucevicius, Katrina Agee, Catherine Bauer, Randy Ferguson, and Dawn Shepherd;

the dedicated bookstore professionals who spent months helping us collect stories;

the parents, grandparents, teachers, and friends who have written the stories included in this book, and the hundreds of others whose work could not be included because of space restrictions.

And, of course, my deepest thanks to my greatest teachers —my parents, Helen and Warren Vannoy, and my children, Emmy and Ali Vannoy.

to the hearts and smiles of children

Contents

10 GREATEST GIFTS

Living and Leading from the Heart

We believe the most powerful force for positive change in the world is within ourselves. The 10 Greatest Gifts Project offers programs, products, and additional tools to help families, organizations, and communities discover and release that power.

Want More Information?

For more information regarding the 10 Greatest Gifts Project, see page 233.

We Love to Hear Your Stories

Nothing brightens our day quite so much as hearing your stories. With your permission we would like to share your experiences with other readers around the country through our 10 Greatest Gifts newsletter or in future books. Please call us at 800-569-1877 or write to: P.O. Box 5301, Denver, CO 80217.

Introduction

I knew I had to write this book almost as soon as my first book, *The 10 Greatest Gifts I Give My Children*, was published in September 1993. Hundreds and then thousands of calls and letters started pouring into my office. Many of the most touching and meaningful were accounts from people who reported that their greatest gifts were not what they had given *to* children but what they had received *from* children.

Some readers found life-altering messages in a simple pair of red socks or a child's kiss or two used horseshoes. Lessons about life were found in the middle of a toddler tussle or a full-blown teenage rebellion. For many, inspiration came at the moment of birth; for others, at the time of a young person's death.

All of the stories chosen for inclusion here depict both powerful and tender episodes when lives stood still for a moment as a child created a new realm of thought or action. The book is rich with diversity and cross-generational ties. Stories have come from mothers and fathers, grandparents, aunts and uncles, teachers, youth leaders, baby-sitters—and even from children themselves. Their messages are about the truth, wonderment, and simple, pure wisdom that come from the hearts of children. All the stories illustrate an understanding of what life and family and community are truly about.

My own daughters, Emmy and Ali, are thirteen and eleven now, and I have finally come to realize that they are—and always have been—my greatest teachers. They constantly create a challenging "classroom" for me in which I can learn and grow when I am willing to unwrap and treasure the gifts they offer. Clearly children are our bridge to the future. But could they also be our bridge to the past? We've spent centuries looking for the fabled fountain of youth; maybe it's located right down the hall.

I have learned that through our children we can discover how to restore our own childlike sense of wonder. Equally as important, however, is to learn not to stifle our children's essence but instead to encourage and nurture it. Even with the best of intentions in the world, adults often destroy the innocence and joy of childhood. Or as a good friend of mine once said, "Children do what's natural until we teach them what's normal."

I also know that kids can be a hassle. There are many tough and trying moments. They make mistakes as they learn and grow. They constantly "push our buttons" and test our limits. Of course they are a responsibility, but they provide us with many wonderful opportunities to see the world through their eyes, to relearn life's most important lessons, and to share the wisdom that seems to come so naturally to them. When we take full advantage of the gifts our children offer us, problems tend to fade away and families blossom.

I am grateful to the many people who have shared the wisdom and beauty of the gifts their children have given to them at the most meaningful moments of their lives. Their stories have enhanced my life, and I hope that you, too, will sip from this book as you would savor a fine wine, for in it are the truths of the universe and the finest expressions of love we may ever know—straight from the hearts and souls of children.

—**Steven W. Vannoy**

CHAPTER ONE

Unwrapping the Gifts

Then a Superhero Comes Along
Debbie Frampton
Levittown, New York

As a preschooler I wanted to be able to move faster than a speeding bullet or leap tall buildings in a single bound, just for the fun of it. In elementary school, when the other kids bullied me, I wished I could spit tiny sticky webs out of my fingers like Spiderman to wrap them up and keep them out of my face. As a teenager I wanted to twirl around three times and have a body to die for like Wonder Woman.

During college I got married and gained a fresh appreciation for superpowers. I would have jumped into the nearest phone booth if I knew I could do a quick change like Superman, to dissect literature and compose brilliant works of undergraduate profundity in a flash. Mostly I needed something to hang on to my extra-mile mentality and leap the barriers keeping me from being all that I could be—by turns a domestic goddess, a woman of substance, a sex kitten, a natural woman, a woman of the '90s, a woman on the go, "every woman."

Who was every woman? Certainly not me. When I was a domestic goddess I dropped into bed mumbling, "Not tonight, honey, I need a catnap." And when I was feeling frisky, my husband would have to shove half-folded clothes off the bed onto the floor to get the job done. It took me an hour to look like a natural woman, and even one thousand sit-ups a day and silicone wouldn't give me a body like Wonder Woman.

When I had my first daughter, Tatum, I had a clear idea of what to expect because I'd read a lot and watched a lot of TV during my twenty-seven years. There would be sleepless nights, stretch marks, and sagging body parts. What I didn't know was that along with all those things, my baby would bring me a gift I'd been wanting all my life: a superpower. I began noticing my new superpower during Tatum's first few days of life. This tiny little bundle of baby nuzzling against me nursing filled me with more contentment than I had ever felt. By the time Tatum was five months old, my whole perspective on life had changed due to my new superpower.

You see, Tatum had given me X-ray vision. She'd smile up at me with her shiny eyes, and I could see right through all of my vain ambition to be "every woman."

It was my perception of what "every woman" was that had blurred my vision. This little spirit who reached for me and touched my face with her little fingers gave me the ability to see that a natural woman is an attitude, not a trend.

So I didn't have the body of Wonder Woman. Oh, well. So I couldn't accomplish tasks faster than a speeding bullet. Big deal. So my house got cluttered, and I didn't wear leather teddies. So what? A woman of the '90s didn't have to be everything to everyone. A woman of substance didn't have to conform to clichés about what women should be.

This superpower was inside me all along, and I didn't even know it until Tatum came along.

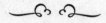

Children, whether our own or those we encounter along our way, create an exhilarating new opportunity for our own transformation and growth. They offer us the chance to learn the lessons we missed before: of how to live, love, play, and forgive.

Their marvelous sense of wonder and sheer excitement in living remind me to look at each new day, even every minute, with a renewed enthusiasm.

Their innate sense of love and compassion and acceptance inspire me to engage in life at a new, expanded level.

Their love of learning and their courage to keep trying encourage me to keep asking, keep daring, and always take one more step toward my goal.

Their natural instinct to forgive reminds me to let go of old, negative patterns and actions.

The sheer beauty and magic of children's true essence give me the only reason I need to greet every day as another peek into the magic and mystery we call life.

When we respond to the opportunities that children provide, we can learn to reengage in life, to get unstuck from doing things the same old way, repeating old miseries, keeping ourselves deprived of hope and dreams.

Grandparents particularly understand this. Across the country, they tell me almost in unison that a grandchild brings a new spark of life and love into their lives, a second chance to be renewed, to make a difference in the world. Children give us one of the most precious gifts we can ever receive—an invitation to learn and grow and bloom ourselves in a classroom unlike any we've ever known.

What if in this classroom you could explore learning in a whole new way? No tests? No lists? No meaningless homework? And where there's always an opportunity for another chance and no failure because you always proceed at your own pace.

What about an education with no tuition, no commuting, no schedules, no degree requirements?

What about a school where you can have recess all day long if you want—and the teacher plays and celebrates right along with you?

What about a teacher who is fun and forgiving, and a classroom where you can look into the teacher's eyes and find love and acceptance unmatched by any other guide on earth?

What about a learning space where you can let your spirit soar, where you don't have to stay quiet, where your ideas and feelings and needs count, where you can laugh and sing and dance and love as much as you want?

What about an education that will result in your evolution, transformation, and growth, that will allow your children to keep their essence, that will empower you to learn to love?

And what if, above all else, the lessons you learn offer you a code of life, a reason for living?

And a Little Child Shall Lead Them
Karen Rae Franklin
Chandler, Arizona

"Thank you, Lord, for this gift of a child. Now I can get on with my life . . . and drink again."

This was my prayer as my newborn was laid in my arms. Looking down at this tiny life, he miraculously appeared to be fine.

I had had dreams of becoming a stewardess, a wife, a mother —and perhaps someday I would write children's stories. I don't recall wanting to be an alcoholic. At the age of twelve, with the innocence of a child and the curiosity of a teenager, I picked up my first drink. It wasn't my last and marked the beginning of the nightmare I lived the next half of my life.

Now twenty-four and eight months sober, I remembered the day I learned I was pregnant. Well-meaning friends, family, and loved ones suggested I end the pregnancy. There was no way I could bring a healthy child into the world in my condition. My hands quaked and my body wracked in shakes as it screamed for alcohol. Doctors asked how in the world I would hold and feed a baby. I wondered the same thing.

I bargained with God for the duration of my pregnancy, begging and pleading with Him to give me a beautiful, healthy child. I promised I would never drink again if He would just grant me this one request. And when it turned out eight months later that God *had* kept His end of the bargain, I somehow felt that I had won. I couldn't wait to get home and get on with life. I could drink again!

But sometime in the early morning hours, my crying newborn was laid in my arms. Nurses told me he was irritable and that maybe I could calm him. Cradling him to my breast I was able to do so. I drifted off to sleep, with rest eluding me as thoughts of drinking crowded my mind. I heard a baby crying in the background and thought to myself, That poor baby . . . someone should pick him up.

It seemed as if hours had passed when I was awakened again, this time by doctors. My little one had been transferred to the intensive care nursery because he had a fever and was extremely irritable. I lay there tossing and turning, not knowing what to do, consumed with fear. I had purposely skipped reading "those pages" when preparing for childbirth. I now wondered if the screams I had heard earlier were those of my child.

When I could stand it no longer, I tiptoed down the hall in search of the nursery. Little did I know that what I would see would change the course of my life forever. Tiny babies, some very sick, others barely hanging on to life, filled the nursery. In the middle was my son, still beautiful and so big in comparison to the others. Motherly instinct drew me to him. I looked down and saw that IVs poked him from head to toe. His little body was bruised and pierced, surely because of me. I stood there crying desperately, thinking, My God, what have I done?

For a moment the world stood still. All the people who had tried so desperately to help me realize a life of sobriety flashed before my eyes. I saw myself as I really was, selfish and self-centered. For the first time in my twenty-four years I saw life as a precious gift.

Doctors never did determine what was wrong with my son

in those early morning hours following his birth. But I knew: There was something wrong with me. Two births occurred that day—mine and his. Thirteen sober years later, I still thank God each day for this child who gave me life—the greatest gift of all.

H eed this warning all ye who enter here! This is not a classroom for the faint of heart or spirit. It is a place with a few very strict requirements—ones that will involve courage, risk-taking, painful discoveries, healing, forgiveness, change, tears, messes and smells and bruises, and, yes, some sleepless nights.

To learn the lessons taught in this classroom we must be willing to take responsibility for ourselves and open up to new ideas, new patterns. When we have children, we embark on a journey where there's no turning back even though we don't know the destination. While this can be a tough journey, if we're willing to step into this classroom with our eyes and ears and hearts wide open, children can, as the saying goes, "teach us to dance as if nobody is watching, to work as if we don't need the money, and to love as if we've never been hurt."

It was a day that mounting evidence of aging plagued both my body and mind. My knees still hurt after hiking down the steep trail in our valley the day before, my hair was receding and thinning, and my energy level was not up to par. In my office I stared blankly at my computer screen, struggling with every word.

Suddenly Emmy and Ali poked their heads through the door, baseball gear in hand. "Let's play some ball," they chorused.

My voice was weary. "I'm pretty tired, but I'll give it a few minutes." I might be aging, I thought, but at least I am not intractable.

Within ten minutes I was playing baseball in a field near our house with the girls and Wister, our black Labrador retriever. Between pitches, Emmy pointed at the late afternoon sky, rapidly changing from pinks to purples to grays and dark blues. Ali noticed the lake two hundred feet below us —its reflection a shimmering copy of the sky but in even softer tones.

I started to look around, too. After a brief afternoon shower, endless varieties of wild flowers and grasses were especially vibrant in shades of yellow, red, lavender, and green. The air was fresh and fragrant. A buckskin-colored doe and her fawn were grazing at the mouth of our wooded valley, not more than three hundred feet away.

We were getting silly. Ali started it with rhymes about the funny-looking batter. Emmy added nonsensical rhymes of her own and physical antics to match. We had been chasing the long fly balls ourselves, but eventually we got too giddy even to run. We asked Wister to retrieve our long hits. He would wait patiently for the crack of the bat, then tear out to pick up each ball and faithfully deposit it at the pitcher's feet. He loved getting in on the game.

Evening arrived too soon. The colors had become soft and muted. It was too dark to see the pitches. Though we wished it would stay light longer, we knew it was time to head home. As we started up the path, a warm little hand slipped into each of mine. I could hardly remember feeling a deeper sense of love and contentment.

We were halfway home when we saw giant irrigation sprinklers come on in a large field to our right. A half-second later the girls asked if they could play in the sprinklers.

My mind was already cataloging all the reasons why they shouldn't: It was getting late, the temperature was dropping, they would get soaked and muddy, it would create more work when we got home. But I stopped when I saw the excitement on their faces. I'd seen that look before, but where? A hazy image lurked in a corner of my memory.

"Okay," I said. "Go for it."

They ran squealing toward the sprinklers, with Wister right behind. I smiled.

Still trying to bring that memory into focus, I began to feel a strange, urgent tingling that I couldn't identify. On impulse I dropped the gloves, bat, and ball. For once in my life I ignored the little voice in my head that didn't want me to let go. I was unstoppable, splashing, squishing, getting soaked to the bone. For a second the look on my daughters' faces was one of pure shock. "Daddy?"

When I paused to watch their vibrant, joyful expressions, that hazy memory suddenly came into focus. I could clearly see my own happy face at the eight of eight, playing in the sprinklers with my brothers on our Nebraska farm—mud oozing through my toes up to my ankles, darting through the milo stalks, mudballs flying and laughter flowing.

We went back to the house, and the wet clothes and mud were no big deal. And there I realized what a priceless gift my daughters had given me—a few moments of my own childhood.

Once upon a Rainbow
Catherine Bauer
Morrison, Colorado

Once upon a time, in the long ago and far away of the mind of every adult there dwelt a fresh and splendorous imagination. It allowed each of us to transform tricycles into dirigibles and those we loved into warm, cozy bundles of comfort. It created playmates for lonely days and sped us via land, air, and sea to the capricious land of make-believe.

It was a time before you bartered with scientific reason, trading the subjective genuine for the objective real. Anything was possible, yet you questioned everything. Let's think twice before we issue the timeworn ultimatum, "Grow up!" Of course, there's a lot to be said for maturity, but there's great advantage, too, in keeping alive that child who is father of the man.

Who else has a sense of wonder that is so magnificent? A butterfly, a singing bird, or a field of grass was once cause for celebration. A leaf, a rock, or a crooked stick was a treasure to be cherished and carted home. Every minute was a moment.

That's not to say tomorrow lacked splendor. Remember what it was like to look forward to something? I mean really look forward to something, with excitement and joy? Nothing's very special anymore. My dad told me when he was a kid ice cream was an annual treat to enjoy each Fourth of July. The day was once special to me, too. It meant a full day of celebrating at Fireman's Park followed by a fireworks finale. Sleep was hard to come by the night before.

In all your yesternights, was there ever one half as exciting as Christmas Eve? Every child makes Christmas Christmas. It was ever so.

What in the world happens to our senses as we grow older? The wearing out isn't nearly so sad as losing the keen edge of glee, that which Wordsworth called the "visionary gleam." Kids taste, smell, feel, and see far better than you or I. And the sixth sense? It was never more finely honed. You can't hoodwink a child.

I harbor in my brain some super-special smells that would hardly twitch a nasal hair today. Take watermelon. On a hot summer evening we carried thick, juicy slices to the old screened porch. It didn't just taste terrific and feel wet and slurpy to the tongue; it smelled cool and clean, refreshing, like Mama's phlox after a shower, except you wouldn't want to eat rain-soaked flowers. I wondered why they didn't make watermelon-flavored ice cream, Jell-O, candy, or pop. But then it might have lost its delicious distinctiveness. It could have become as ordinary as orange or strawberry.

When Mother tossed pork hocks and cabbage into a big kettle, the ambrosial aroma told me that my favorite dinner was on the way. Now I cook cabbage with a vent fan roaring while spraying the kitchen with "Misty Glen" from an aerosol can.

As well as I remember carving the toothy grin in my jack-o'-lantern, I remember the damp, earthy smell of fresh pumpkin and the way the odor changed when smoke from the lighted candle blackened the pumpkin lid.

They say smell best triggers recollection, but there was no sound more comforting than the mournful whistle of the old steam locomotive each night around ten. I sank into my feather tick and listened to that mournful, faraway lullaby. As it melted into the stillness of the night, it left behind an all-is-right-with-the-world comfort and calm.

If we weren't so conditioned to what we label the ordinary, we would continue to marvel at trifles. Children see mysterious patterns in leafy branches, marshmallow clouds, and wood grain on a door. Color was never as vibrant as when you were four. That's mostly why kids love balloons, suckers, blocks, picture books, and fire engines. That's why they paint bright yellow suns, deep purple lions, and rainbows across the sky.

Once you didn't run in and out of the rain under a bubble umbrella. You welcomed it with open arms, head tipped to the sky, feet sloshing in a puddle. You felt its wetness, saw its crystal-line beauty, smelled its freshness. The only way to improve upon it was to turn nature's thermostat down a few notches and catch snowflakes on your tongue.

One day when a storm threatened, my mother didn't buy my excuse for being late coming from school. I had walked extra blocks just to feel the powerful wind pushing my back, lifting my feet, magically propelling me.

The wetness of worms on a fishhook, the coolness of sand on bare toes, the mushiness of mud pies on stubby little fingers would never feel today as they did when the world was new and filled with wonder.

When I taught children's art classes, far more than I taught them, they taught me. Children are spontaneous, creative, filled with joy. (A paradox to ponder: Sheer joy fires creativity in a child; when he matures, it takes pain to do the same.) Kids have no hang-ups, no stereotyped notions of how it ought to be. They cut, paint, sculpt, and draw with sureness and vigor. If a picture doesn't look well right side up, they'll tip it sideways or upside down. Newly inspired, they'll work from there. What began as a crooked house turns into a kite. Clouds metamorphose into flower gardens.

Third-grader Bobby, unhappy with his efforts, in a burst of frustration crumpled his painting. As I was about to comment, out of shame or curiosity, he timidly unfolded the sheet of manila paper. The exciting explosion of melding colors was rivaled only by his smile of joy-filled surprise. A nubby-textured area burst forth where paints pulled from one another, leaving tiny points of pigment. Marbleized blends filled one corner. Crinkles caused by crushing provided a batik effect.

"Whee!" he cried impulsively, and his creation held high was the center of attention. Everyone wanted to try. Why not? How many works of art and work-saving inventions do you suppose were born by happenstance?

We mounted the paintings on black construction paper.

What a stir the hall display created. "How could they do it?" "Such expressions of delight!" "Third graders, incredible!" Teachers asked to buy the treasures.

When a little Jimmy or Marie thrusts forth a dandelion bouquet, I am moved to wonder if in all the world there is a wisdom as great as kindness. A child possesses a beautiful innocence that is not simply the naiveté of not knowing but rather a precious and rare kind of optimism, honesty, openness, and trust. If you fear frankness, you'd best not communicate with one who has not yet learned to worry about impressing others.

A kid doesn't try to keep up with the Joneses. Indeed, his plan of action seems to say, Life is too exciting, exploring the earth too wondrous, to allow other people to live my life for me.

Yet how difficult it becomes to keep a sense of openness (it means remaining vulnerable); of freedom, fun, and laughter; of wonder and of joy . . . for inevitably, life is tragic. As we listen to the still, sad music of humanity, one day we come to regard earthly existence with stunned pity and silent awe.

How sad the poignant truth that adults must forcibly think in order to bring back, even in memory, that consciousness which is second nature to a child! I stand with Holden Caulfield. Of all the things that I could be, I'd like most to be a Catcher in the Rye. To keep the child happily alive in you and me . . . what greater calling could there be?

CHAPTER TWO

The Gift of Presence

❧

A Walk on the Child Side
Laura A. Ruel-Rella
Omaha, Nebraska

It was one of those days. The stifling heat of another 100-plus-degree Nebraska day seemed to penetrate right through the walls of my house and intensify the moods of my children. The cries of Allie, my teething toddler, and the endless questions and requests from Amy, my curious four-year-old, had turned my mind to mush. My white shorts were stained with Kool-Aid, the playroom carpet was covered in Play-Doh, and my kitchen counter was washed in watercolors.

As the dinner hour approached, I watched Amy pick up the dripping, defrosted package of chicken to contemplate our entree, while Allie created a trail of uncooked rice as she toddled about, hugging the open bag. I gave up. Everyone just seemed too antsy, and peace was a concept too foreign to fathom. All I could do was count the seconds until my relief worker (a.k.a. my husband) reported for duty.

Finally, I heard his car. The moment I saw him, I grabbed the dog's leash and made a beeline for the door.

"I'm walking the dog tonight—alone," I firmly stated, my teeth clenched. My replacement knew better than to ask why.

"Have a nice walk," he shouted as I hurried away.

Once outside, I took a deep breath and marveled at how peaceful a street busy with playing children and passing cars could be. Our dog led me along our regular route. Good, I thought, I won't even have to think about which way to go.

I swung my arms, feeling unencumbered and free. This walk was a daily ritual, but usually I did it while pushing a weighty double stroller and responding to Allie's mumblings and Amy's constant chatter.

Tonight, I thought, this walk is *all mine*.

My pace picked up, and I began to look around. There was that familiar hole in the sidewalk that I always lugged the heavy stroller around. Not tonight, I thought, and stepped over it with ease.

But what was that? It was as though I heard something. . . . Oh, yes, it was my girls. Whenever I maneuvered that sidewalk hole, they would sing in unison, "Whoa . . . whoa!" They called that spot the "Whoa Corner."

I stopped. I smiled. Suddenly I turned back, walked around that hole, and said, "Whoa!"

The all-too-common thunder of jets from a nearby airstrip roared overhead. Now it was Allie I envisioned, pointing her pudgy little index finger in the air and enthusiastically bopping up and down in her seat, squealing, "Up-plane. Up-plane!"

And then it was imaginative Amy: "Where is it going, Mommy? Where? Is it heading toward Jaci's house in California, or is it going to see John Raymond in Massachusetts?"

I began to slow down. "Sit," I said to the dog, aiming his nose toward the sky. "See the airplane," I said and wondered where it was going. California, I decided. I wondered who was on it: business people, families, lovers. I imagined I was on it, heading toward Napa Valley and a cozy little inn.

We resumed our walk and rounded another corner onto a main road. PRIME COMMERCIAL REAL ESTATE, the familiar sign shouted at me. The empty overgrown lot, seemingly a dump site for some customers of the neighboring McDonald's, hastened my return from Napa Valley.

An untied shoe caused me to stop and bend down. Before I stood up, I looked straight ahead. "My meadow," Amy's sweet voice offered.

Only a child could see a meadow in this lot of garbage, my mind responded. I looked again. You know, I thought, at stroller height this lot does look different. All at once I noticed the tall grasses, the wild flowers, the twisting vines. A meadow? Maybe.

I led our reluctant dog onto the lot and immediately began picking bouquets of wild flowers. The colors were spectacular— purple, pink, yellow. As my arms became overloaded I found myself wishing I had a basket to hold more.

I raced home so quickly that our dog could barely keep up. I burst into the house, ran to my children, and gave them each a bouquet and a hug.

"How was your walk, Mommy?" they asked.

"It was nice," I said. "But it's best when you are with me."

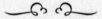

At times, as an adult, we get so buried in to-do lists, resentments, pain, and fears. One more messy diaper to change, another sticky table to clean, another trip to the grocery store—our lives are sometimes so cluttered with daily junk that we simply forget to see the wonder and enchantment of life that children feel so naturally. How much would we gain in balance and perspective just by getting back to that magic for even a few minutes a day?

Sweet Serenity
Pamela Blount
Waterford, Michigan

Christmas greeted me at 6:00 A.M. with the soft cry of my new daughter, Samantha. The day I anticipated had arrived. My husband and I would proudly introduce our three-week-old baby to many of our family and friends for the very first time.

I cradled Samantha in one arm and fed her as we rocked in front of the Christmas tree. There was an ornament in my direct view with the inscription SAMANTHA'S FIRST CHRISTMAS. I stared at the words and then back at my beautiful baby. That visual combination reinforced a thought that I returned to each day: This is really happening. I am a mother! This is my baby!

Samantha closed her eyes and went into another peaceful slumber. I placed her into her crib, walked out, returned, and considered placing her right back in my arms. She looked so comfortable I didn't dare. I set out her clothes. I made the decision to buy her a white dress with red lace ribbon the instant I spotted it. If she were dressed in a plain frock, it would have made no difference to Samantha. I knew that. I wanted her dress to be very special, though. I would carefully pack it away so that years later we could look at it together and hold it in our hands as I described our first Christmas together.

When Samantha awoke again, my husband did, too. Together we bathed and dressed our little Christmas baby. "A bow," my husband said. "Let's put a bow in her hair." He twirled a small portion of her fine, wispy hair together and held it in position until I had the little red ribbon secured. We spent the next hour just looking at Samantha, watching even her most subtle movements in amazement.

The three of us ventured out. I looked forward to having Samantha feel the warmth of the people in our lives, the people she would come to love and who would love her in return. It was wonderful. There were presents and feasts and more presents and even more feasts. Throughout, Samantha was in someone's arms. But I will always remember the images from the wee hours of that morning by the tree, with Samantha and later with my husband, getting ready for Christmas, with no presents, no feast, just us.

I guess we weren't getting ready for Christmas at all. No, we were having Christmas right then. And that's the greatest gift my child has ever given me—the capacity to recognize endearing moments derived from life itself. It's a quality I didn't possess prior to her birth. Happiness was mostly episodic for me —the next job promotion, party, or vacation. I now know that happiness can be quieter and more enduring than all that. I just needed a nine-pound miracle to discover a sweet serenity that once eluded me.

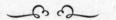

Sometimes our minds are so fixated on the past or in the future that we only truly experience 50 percent of the day. Children invite us to come back home, to be here in the moment. Every time we are not fully engaged in the moment is time we have lost forever.

It's a priceless lesson to watch children, especially babies, simply experience their feelings, let them out with screams or giggles, and then refocus on whatever the next moment brings. What would the difference be in your life if you could be "present" just 10 percent more each day?

My daughter Emmy gave me that priceless gift not long ago.

The minute she saw the Häagen-Dazs sign, I felt a slight tug at my arm and a faster pace for our feet. But as soon as we stepped inside the store, her pace slowed dramatically. Her eyes gleamed with anticipation. Her nose twitched. Her body language shouted pure excitement.

Since the store was empty and the clerk loved children, Emmy could travel at her own pace. She considered every flavor, tasted multiple samples, and carefully supervised the clerk's skillful hands as she shaped and formed her chosen cone.

Emmy knows how to savor things. She gently licked the ice cream, shaped it with her tongue, and then sat back with eyes half closed to let the pleasure soak in. Watching Emmy treasure her treat was the most *I* have ever enjoyed an ice-cream cone.

I wondered what it would be like if I could learn to savor parts of my life just as deeply. Three days later I tried it with a friend of mine. The subject: a chicken chimichanga. We took our time and savored every bite. The crisp taco, the smooth sour cream, the crunchy lettuce, the tongue-tingling "pico de gallo" salsa—I had never known there were so many separate tastes and textures in something I normally just wolfed down. A chimichanga had never tasted so good. We left refreshed, peaceful, happy—and full.

I applied Emmy's savoring technique the next day with another friend on a forest hike. Our steps were slower, our eyes open wider. We stopped often to consider scents, colors, and sounds. Our mood extended to a deeper consideration of all our words, thoughts, and feelings. We were right there with every bit of woodland flora and fauna, smells and textures, sights and sounds.

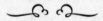

Ice cream, chimichangas, forests—everything is here for us to savor *now*. We don't have to own something to appreciate it. And think about all the things we do own that we have stopped savoring and appreciating. As my friend had noted on our woodland walk, ownership doesn't guarantee appreciation, and appreciation doesn't require ownership. Appreciation is a choice—our choice. I wonder how many of us have children whom we really don't know because we don't appreciate them for themselves. Too often we try to make them into the children we want them to be rather than loving them for the children they are.

The following story tells of a moment of childhood innocence when a mother learned to appreciate that her son did not have to do everything "right," and she could forgo what is often a false sense of how important some things are. She could forget the rules and simply savor the moment.

Holy Ghostbusters
Terri Reid
Lena, Illinois

Sundays have always presented a challenge to teach our children the importance of reverence during church. We want a balance between realistic expectations and some kind of acknowledgment that during this time we should be trying to remember we are in church. Part of the compromise has been paper, crayons, and pencils. This way the children can draw and sit still for a little while.

As the children get older, we ask them to try to listen to the speakers because they might actually learn something. Imagine my pride when Nathan, who was then four, showed me his picture of the Holy Ghost, the topic the speaker was discussing. As the picture progressed, I noted that he was drawing another couple of figures.

"Who are they?" I asked.

"Oh, they're the ghostbusters, and they're going to bust the Holy Ghost!"

Oh well!

Nathan taught me about humor that day. And he also reminded me that the Heavenly Father must have a great sense of humor, too, and we should spend more time enjoying life and less worrying about silly things.

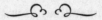

The following poignant story was told by a mother of five who realized how many important moments she had allowed to slip away over her children's lifetimes.

No Label for Love
Val Croll
Steamboat Springs, Colorado

Now it's the '90s, and there are nifty labels to help me better understand my family during the '50s. There are plenty of labels that might have applied to my ex-husband and me: dreamy, creative, alcoholic, manic depressive, compulsive, obsessive, codependent, workaholic, and probably many more, useful only to our mean-spirited acquaintances. The children had labels, too: little mother, guru, peacekeeper, little princess, personality kid, and an assortment of adjectives that might have applied depending on their stage of development.

Ah, yes, then there's the dreaded label: middle child. That would have been Kim. (See, you thought I forgot him!) He was our good-natured charmer. But he was also "lost in the shuffle" and "gone to the neighbors a lot."

This strong, beautiful boy, now a man, with blond hair and deep brown eyes, always seemed happy and full of life. Now it has been suggested that he was just covering for chronic sadness and extreme loneliness. I was informed recently that he spent most of his childhood away from home! All I know is that he appeared regularly at the dinner table, the second kid on my left.

All my children, to this day, accuse me of having no memory

at all. Endless days of washing, ironing, cleaning, cooking, chauffeuring, gardening, entertaining, and counseling would have used up my total memory bank! And then there was the full-time job at the state hospital as a psychiatric nurse, which was successfully designed to accommodate my spare time.

When Kim was a senior in high school, his father and I were divorced. "A matter of mathematics," I told him. "Nothing personal. Either seven of us will go down the tube, or six of us have a chance." The two oldest children were on their own, so when I got a better paying job in another town, I left with only Kim and his two younger siblings.

Though just a family of four now, my new job was a killer! I was the first psych nurse in the state to become a director of an outpatient mental health clinic, and my catchment area included three huge rural counties, covering ten thousand square miles. I was traveling so much that I found myself grateful in the knowledge that old friends of the family, mainly teenage friends of Kim's, would visit nearly every weekend, especially in the winter when they came to ski. But even after graduating from high school, Kim ended up living at home periodically, and his young adult friends continued to visit.

One particular weekend, Kim's friends were due to gather, and I warned him that I was under a lot of pressure on the job, preparing for an important seminar, and I didn't need any extra hassle. Enough said!

That Friday I left at sunrise and returned home at two in the morning, knowing that my aching, exhausted body had to survive two more days of supreme effort. I opened the door on a lively scene. Kim and several of his merry friends were at the dining room table, laughing loudly, smoking, drinking, and quite possibly being a trifle illegal. They greeted me with an enthusiasm I did not share!

I remember a ball of anger rising up in my throat. I could see a black aura emanating from my taut body. And from the sudden silence, I think Kim's friends saw it, too. Kim, however, was intent on being sociable, and leaping to his feet, he shouted,

"Hey, Mom, you've got to sit down and visit with us!" In a threatening, cold tone, and with a murderous look, I replied, "There's only one thing I have to do and that's get some sleep!"

As I stumbled down the hall I heard Kim call out, "That's garbage! You never have time for us kids. You're always too busy!"

All my children are adults now, with their own children. I live alone. My life no longer centers around survival. I pronounced myself "retired" recently, and to celebrate my new status I have been known to turn my back on a sink full of dirty dishes and join friends for a very leisurely lunch. We laugh, talk, share, and are sometimes quiet and serious.

When there's a lull in the conversation, I indulge in my favorite fantasy: It's forty years ago. I'm seated on the floor, leaning against a hamper of laundry. Kim is sprawled at my feet, studying his toy train. The white, wrinkled thumb on his right hand is tucked safely in his puckered mouth. The chubby fingers of his left hand pull at the tight blond ringlets at the nape of his neck. There's nothing being said. No need.

Not every lesson we learn from our children is pleasurable or easy to grasp. Sometimes it is a painful one; sometimes our regrets teach us what is truly important.

Rock Me One More Time
Katrina Agee
Englewood, Colorado

It had started out as a pretty average mid-July day. I was hurrying my three children out the door to Grandma's and some horse-back riding. Serina had a car and could drive herself and her younger sister and brother. It seemed at the time that I had many important things to do at work, and I was irritated that my house and family couldn't somehow be more cooperative and considerate of my schedule. As they all kissed me and said "good-bye," I pointed out that there were rooms to clean up and clothes to fold as soon as they got home that evening.

But that evening turned into an all-night vigil in the emergency room and later the intensive care unit. The doctor's words fell like lead weights, echoing and bouncing off the bright lights and shiny hospital floors: "We'll have to wait and see. . . . Your daughter has a fractured skull and a contracoup brain injury, a result of the blows to her head during the horseback riding accident."

Although the fracture was on the back of her skull, the doctor went on, the injury was on the front of her brain. He tried to sound hopeful, yet he was cautious not to give us too much optimism to go on. "We'll just have to wait and see. . . . Just making it through the next twenty-four hours is the important thing to hope for right now."

All my life I have been surrounded by people who are definite. I didn't like all these vague speculations. I wanted to know that my little girl would be fine and life would go on as usual, with as little disruption as possible.

The hours dragged into days. I slept on the floor next to Serina's hospital bed. I had lots of time to think and hope and pray. It seemed like a good time to relive the past sixteen years of Serina's life. One memory repeated itself over and over again: Serina was three years old, maybe four. I would tuck her into bed and then go downstairs to busy myself with important tasks of the evening—washing dishes, doing laundry, picking up toys. Serina had a hard time going to sleep. She'd yell, "Mommy, rock me. Please rock me."

I'd reply sternly, "No, Serina. Go to sleep. Mommy is busy and has things to do."

"But, Mommy, I need you to rock me. Please rock me."

I rarely gave in while she was awake. One night I felt guilty and carried her down to my rocking chair after she was already asleep. She never knew it, though.

I don't know when she last asked me to rock her. One day, I suppose, she gave up. But now, lying on the floor in the hospital next to my daughter who just couldn't wake up, I longed for her to call out to me, "Mommy, rock me. Please rock me." I would have answered, "Serina, there is nothing more important to me this moment than rocking you. Please let me rock you all night."

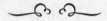

"Thanks be to God," Katrina later reported, "Serina recovered completely, but I'll never be the same again. I'll take time to rock or talk, whatever the need may be."

It still hurts deeply when I think about all the moments I missed with my daughters, all the times when they wanted to hold my hand or hug my knee and I thought I was too busy. We can't ever go back, but we can always start now to appreciate every moment we spend with our children. This anonymous poem helps remind me that it's costly to let these precious moments slip away unnoticed and unappreciated.

> Have you seen anywhere, a dear boy and a girl,
> and their small winsome brother of four?
> It was only today that barefoot and brown they
> played by my kitchen door.
> It was only today or . . .
> maybe a year . . .
> it couldn't be twenty I know . . .
> that laughing and singing they called me to play.
>
> But I was too busy to go . . .
> too busy with finance and homework to play . . .
> and now they've grown up and they've wandered
> away.

Someday I know they must stop and look back . . .
and wish they were children again . . .
and, oh, just to hold them and play once again . . .
I'd run out my kitchen door . . .
for there's never a chore that could keep me away

. . . could I just hear my children call me to play.
Where are my children?
I've got time . . .
today.

—⟋ᘒ ᘓ⟍—

I believe that one of the most important efforts we make for our children is to create a safe place in which they can dance and play, take risks, and be fully in the moment. In return, they will shower us with the gifts of joy and excitement and wonder.

Seize the Moment, Share the Dance
Amy Shore
Branchburg, New Jersey

This morning (as he does every morning) Barney is dancing and singing on television to the delight of my two-year-old daughter, and I sip my juice at the kitchen table watching Miranda's face light up when Barney sings the infamous "I love you/You love me" song. I learn so much from my daughter who truly knows what life is all about. Me with a master's degree and almost thirty years of life experience, she with a thirty-word vocabulary and diaper-covered bottom—together we share day-to-day life. It's wonderful seeing the ordinary through her extraordinary blue eyes.

Miranda loves to sing regardless of how off-key she sounds.

She dances whenever she hears music. And running down a grassy hill on a sunny afternoon makes her giggle. Miranda is never embarrassed when she is naked, and she never tries to hold in a sneeze or a laugh.

When Miranda is happy, she loudly shouts; she doesn't know she should keep her voice down in public places. When Miranda is sad, she loudly cries, tears streaking her soft, round cheeks; she doesn't know that she should keep her disappointments inside until they can be privately vented. She loves and she likes and she shares and she shouts and she plays and she cries and, simply, she lives. Why can't we adults be that uninhibited, that content, that simple, that honest?

When Miranda grows up, I wonder if she will continue to notice how small the ants are on the sidewalk, how high the planes fly in the sky, how soft caterpillar fur feels. Will she remember to say, "I love you just because"? Will she smile, dance, laugh, and cry when she wants to? Most important, will she take the time to enjoy her life? I breathe a loud sigh thinking about all of this. (Miranda thinks I can do anything, and for her I *can* do anything.)

Carpe diem! Seize the day! Seize the moments. I've realized that raising children is life's most important priority, not to be squeezed between going to aerobics class and having the car's oil changed. Miranda shows me that when I remove all the "stuff-to-do" from an ordinary day, I'm amazed at how bright the sky is, how fresh newly cut grass smells, how pretty a dandelion looks, and, sadly, how short life really is. And I hope I will try to keep my child's fascination with the simple beauty of life long after her baby fat has disappeared.

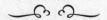

Happily, parents aren't the only recipients of the joy and wonder of life that children offer us. They also give that gift to their grandparents. Love is truly ageless.

Pure and Simple Joy
Frances Bible Bryant
Richmond, Virginia

In just three years my granddaughter Emma has worked a spell on me, an old lady of seventy-two. She transfigures and transforms me; she lifts my spirit. She climbs onto the piano bench and invites me to join her.

"Play, Ma, play," she entreats.

I struggle with the notes, but still, she sings out vigorously. We sing "Jingle Bells" even though it is July. In this brief moment my heart is light.

On rainy days we draw and color with Magic Markers. On my half of the drawing pad I try to impress her with sketches of parks and zoos, houses and landscapes. She is occupied with a giant black circle spinning in the middle of the page.

"It's a storm," she explains even though I haven't asked.

Her creation is more appropriate than anything I've drawn, considering that Felix, a hurricane, has been at our back door for the past few days. I watch as she surveys her work. She seems dissatisfied. After a little reflection, she draws a yellow circle inside the center of the blackness.

"That's the sun," she adds. Now she likes the picture, and so do I.

Our backyard is Gulliver's world, full of both small and large creatures, real and imagined. Emma crouches on the ground to watch the ants parade, mesmerized by this minute spectacle. I, too, am caught up and take time out to witness and marvel.

Emma remembers a story we've just read. Up she jumps and begins to run, waving her arms, swaying her body, turning sharply right, then left. She is the Bad Bull and I am, as directed, the timid Ferdinand. Again I am part of her boundless imaginative world.

We lie on our backs on a pallet under a tree and study today's cottony clouds. I resist volunteering my version of the configurations; instead, I wait for hers. What I have been viewing quickly alters when I hear her version. I have envisioned a dog; she sees Sassy, our old family poodle who died a year ago. We draw roads in the dirt on which to drive her miniature cars and trucks.

"Sit down here, Ma. You can play, too." I am grateful to be included as a participant rather than as a mere observer. So I say to Emma, "You're terrific!"

She counters, "No, no, I'm Emma."

She says she loves me. Me? I am wrinkled and gray. Her arms encircle my neck, and she restores in me something pure and simple—joy and peace.

What's a Grandson?
by Catherine Bauer
Morrison, Colorado

An eye-opener, that's what he is; a fix for frailty, failing eyesight, or faulty hearing; an antidote for apathy, boredom, a case of the blahs. Seeing the world through his two-year-old eyes is nothing short of revelation. How blind we become to unselfconscious wonder as we grow older.

When his mother announced the impending trip from Wisconsin to Colorado to visit Grandma and Grandpa, wide-eyed and laughing, Aaron made one succinct statement, "Wowee!" It turned out to be as much prediction as proclamation.

Just yesterday he sucked in his breath and pointed his finger more times than I could count. "Look, Grandma, a bunny!" Sure enough, I hadn't spotted it camouflaged among the gray-brown rocks and scrubby foliage of our mountainside. There it sat, eyeing us cautiously, inspecting two human creatures who stood very still and stared back.

Aaron thought he spied another rabbit when a squirrel crossed our path. Our Rocky Mountain squirrels are black, and they have what look like long bunny ears but are really extra long hairs that shoot up behind their pointed ears.

"Duck?" Aaron tilted his head and listened to distant quacking. Could be. Ducks populate our Turkey Creek. Yes, very likely, I agreed as I listened carefully.

"Airplane?" He heard a dull roar and sought verification.

"I think it's a truck on Highway 285," I said. Throwing our heads back, we checked above. Right again. A jet chalked a line across the sky.

Another swoosh of air intake, and a fat little paw extended. A bright vermilion butterfly on a dandelion leaf. A brave one, too, for the tiny finger almost anointed the stained-glass wings before they fell open, flapped, and carried their magic on up the hill. "Butterfly, butterfly," Aaron screeched, imploring the creature to stay awhile.

But disappointment is short-lived, for each departing wonder leaves in its wake another. I picked a dandelion and put it under his chin to see if he liked butter. We picked several more of the bright yellow flowers for Mommy and Grandpa—a bright bouquet for the kitchen table. No one told him there are those who dub these golden treasures weeds.

Picking up a pinecone from the drive, he held it up for me to see. "Pinecone," he said. I'd told him once what it was the day before. It's downright reassuring to realize that one of us can remember, but it's disconcerting, too. I thought two-year-olds were for asking "What's that?" and "Why?" and "Why?" some more. And I thought grandmas were for pointing out nature's little miracles, not once but twice, and then twice more.

When we spied a ladybug, we let it crawl on Grandma's finger. This creature, too, he recognized, for it was in the book Grandma made for Christmas. The rhyme, old as time for Grandma, was new to Aaron.

Ladybug, ladybug,
Fly away home.

Your house is on fire, and
Your children will burn.

We hunkered down on the grassy bank of Turkey Creek and launched ships galore, crafts that for all the world resembled sticks and leaves and grass. Grandma had to grab the back of his pants when Aaron leaped forward, squealed, and pointed. Aha, a waterbug! Not just one but four among the reeds near the shore.

The sight of them took me back. As a child they used to fascinate me when I went fishing with my grandmother. The creatures glide, then jerk; float, then stagger.

Aaron called them spiders. "Waterbugs," Grandma corrected.

"Waterbugs," he said, shaking his head in confirmation.

On our walk back up the hill, we shared toting the mail. We had to stop and sometimes squat, the better to watch ants on the driveway. One was dragging a bug. "Why?" I wasn't sure but "for food" was the guess I made.

It's a long driveway, so we played games. When Aaron stood still, I circled around him several times, then hurried on ahead to take my silent stance. He'd paddle up to my spot and trot around me, giggling and squealing all the while, unaware that it was Grandma's ploy to avoid carrying him after he'd stood begging a "ride" with outstretched arms.

We never make it past the propane tank without mounting the monstrosity and together chugging along in our steam engine, or if he grasps his imaginary steering wheel, I know it's a truck he's maneuvering down the busy highway. This time Aaron spurred his wild steed down the trail. "Giddyap, horsie."

Thereafter we crossed the yard to watch the neighbor's real horses. When the collie barked, Aaron leaned against the fence, tilting his head against the post, and began to sing in a wee voice. I crept closer, ear cocked. "Old MacDonald had a farm, ee-i-ee-i-o. On his farm he had a doggie. Woof-woof here. Woof-

woof there. . . . Had a horsie. Neigh-neigh here. Neigh-neigh there. Neigh-neigh everywhere."

Can you believe all those marvelous wonders exploded on one round trip from the house to the mailbox at the foot of the hill? Miracles his grandmother just took for granted.

Wowee!

CHAPTER THREE

The Gift of Perspective

—⚬⚬—

Waiting for the Sunshine
Donna L. Clovis
Princeton Junction, New Jersey

Our family was awakened by the shrieking sound of the alarm at 5:30 on a cold January morning. I started the coffee and began to think about my workday and the ballet lessons I had to take my daughter to after school. It was going to be one of those days, packed with business meetings and activities. But when I peered out my kitchen window I noticed that the trees in our yard were blanketed in white. It had snowed last night—enough, it seemed, to cancel school for the day. I turned on the radio. As I had suspected, schools were closed.

"Kids," I yelled upstairs, "no school today!"

I could hear them shout with joy.

"Oh, no," my husband complained. "That means I have to clean off the car and do the driveway. I'm going to be late!"

By this time everyone was in the kitchen.

"I can't wait to play in the snow, Mommy!" my seven-year-old daughter Michaela screamed.

"And I can't wait, either!" Matt, my nine-year-old son, chimed in. His eyes were large and brimming with excitement. "Come on, Michaela, let's get our boots and snow pants on!

When the sun comes out, we'll be ready to play!" They disappeared upstairs.

"No one said it was going to snow!" my husband said, storming upstairs to get dressed. "I just have so much to do today. And I'm sure the traffic will be hectic, and there's going to be delay after delay. We always have bad weather when I have so much to do!"

It wasn't until later in the morning, when the children were outside playing on their sleds and making snowmen, that it hit me: How often do we adults complain about the weather? It's either too hot or too cold. Or it's rainy or snowy. The weather is something that we can't change, but it seems to put us grownups in a "gray funk," affecting all of our activities all day.

But my two young children had shared something very special with me on that cold January morning. I watched them from the window playing in the snow for hours. They were happy to enjoy whatever weather was given to them. When it was cold and snowing, they took advantage of it by having fun with their sleds. When it rained, they put on their raincoats and boots and found every puddle to splash in. When it was sunny, they would run in the yard playing until they were exhausted. They easily adapted to their situation with a happy and positive attitude.

Why do I keep thinking I have to wait for the sunshine? Let it snow!

A Matter of Perspective
Julie Strong
Waterford, Michigan

Dismayed, I sat on the living room floor, playing with my three-and-a-half-year-old son, Michael, and my six-month-old son, Alex, surrounded by the midmorning clutter of toys. Maybe Michael would play by himself while Alex napped so I could get "something" done, I thought hopefully. My mental to-do list scrolled through my mind: phone calls to make, housecleaning, bills to be paid, article to be written for the preschool newsletter, and other "important" tasks awaiting my attention. Alex and Michael had gotten up early, which eliminated any possibility of a morning beauty routine. Throw in a case of the nothing-exciting-ever-happens-to-me blues, and Mommy was in a very ho-hum mood.

"Ten o'clock already," I mumbled, "and I haven't done anything yet today."

Michael quietly put down his truck, looked me in the eye, and said, "But, Mommy, yes you have. You got Alex up, you helped me get dressed, you made us breakfast, you changed Alex's stinky, we played fire trucks. . . ."

Thank you, Michael, for reminding me of the truly important things.

Children look at things from their own special perspective, which is often quite different from ours but is almost always a revelation.

I remember a cold December Colorado day when Ali, Emmy, and I were walking out of a shopping mall. Ali and I were visibly shivering and shaking as we rushed quickly toward the car. Emmy seemed to be in no hurry and didn't even appear cold. And she wasn't wearing a coat.

"Emmy, aren't you freezing?" I yelled.

"No, this feels good," she replied.

When we were in the Jeep and I was warm enough to control my chattering teeth, I probed a little deeper. "Ali and I were freezing, Emmy, and you weren't even cold. What's going on?"

Her reply: "I have chosen to like that feeling."

I was confused. "What in the world do you mean?"

"Who says that feeling cold has to be bad?" she said. "I have chosen to like it, and now I do like it. Feeling cold feels good to me."

Emmy's words got me thinking. I was glad that we were quiet on the drive home. I remembered that Benjamin Franklin had taught himself to sleep on a bare bed without a blanket in a cold room and actually enjoyed it. But I, like many people, have always associated cold with feeling uncomfortable. Was it possible that I could associate it with a good feeling? Maybe I could even do the same thing with my dislike of hot weather.

Just seven months later I left an air-conditioned movie theater during a July heat wave, walked out into the sunshine, and smiled. I realized it was working. As I climbed into my Jeep, I actually felt embraced and nurtured by the sun-warmed air. I sent another silent thank-you to that "teacher who lives down the hall." Emmy had taught me that I can either be a slave to my mind or I can make it my servant. It is my choice, and that changes everything.

Not Even a Millimeter Higher
(A story told to me by a participant in one of my 10 Greatest Gifts seminars who had to catch a ride before I could identify him.)

I guess persistence really does pay off. My wife, Ruth, and I had been firm on the "No dog" decision, but now the whole family was on the way to the pound.

Our reluctance gradually turned to excitement as we listened to our children in the backseat. Dreams of playing ball, cuddling, and a loyal watchdog punctuated the conversation. Potential names ranged from Rover to Mac. (They had already decided on a boy.) The name debate had started to turn into a shouting match when we passed Sammie's Chow Chinese Restaurant. Ruth pointed at the restaurant sign. "How about that name?" All six eyes in the backseat locked onto the big red Sammie sign, and the name was official.

At the pound, Ruth and I decided to stand back and let the kids gravitate toward the dog they naturally fell in love with. We breathed a big sigh of relief when they walked by the big black Great Dane mixed with more varieties than Heinz. But then they headed back that way, and our five-year-old daughter, Susie, stopped at his cage. There was a friendly woof and a wag of the tail, and Susie called for Chelsea, her fifteen-year-old sister. After two more woofs and a lick, they motioned for their twelve-year-old brother, David.

We responded to their choice with three well-aimed parental counterattacks to try to convince the kids otherwise: "He's too big to cuddle with. He'll cost too much to feed. He'll do bigger doodles." But our strategy fell on deaf ears, so Ruth and I decided to stick to our original "fall-in-love-gravitate" decision.

We started to have second thoughts when we tried to stuff our new 120-pound dog into our minivan. The good news was that he was good-natured about it, and he had a flexible neck. The bad news was when we stopped at Pet City to stock up on the recommended dog food, supplies, and requisite toys. I'm sure that if I had seen the $145 total before we went to the pound, Sammie would not have had the chance to join the Myer family.

As we approached the minivan after our shopping expedition, you'd think the kids were being reunited with a long-lost family member. Everyone, even Ruth, was hysterically happy. But barely two blocks up the road, Chelsea let out a heart-stopping shriek: "I think Sammie had an accident on the seat and I sat right in it."

Sure enough, both the seat and Chelsea's dress were stained. So we swerved around and went back to Pet City to spend another $25 on Sammie clean-up supplies. Of course, Ruth and I did our very best to keep our cool and set a calm and dignified example for the kids. Little did we know that our dignified act was about to be completely shattered.

We pulled into the garage as usual, and each of us began to carry one or two bags up the entryway steps toward the kitchen. In the meantime, Sammie bounded through the open door and quickly made himself at home. I entered the kitchen just in time to see Sammie, paws on the kitchen counter, tail in full wag, completing his mid-morning snack. He had just polished off two loaves of Ruth's freshly baked bread!

In a nutshell, he was uncontrollable and unteachable. In three more days he had dug up half the backyard, growled at several neighbor kids, and left giant muddy paw prints all over the house. Ruth and I knew we were in over our heads and had begun to discuss returning the flawed merchandise.

A few mornings later we awoke to a new disaster: Sammie had ripped a couch cushion into a million pieces and spread the stuffing all over the house. All dignity was now shattered. I went ballistic. I assembled the kids to break the news as gently as my anger would allow. "That damn dog is going back to the pound right now!"

I expected and received buckets of pleas and tears, but I was committed to following the first rule of parenting: Do not waver in your decisions. I tried to ease their pain. I reminded Susie of the Pocahontas doll that Sammie had eaten, David of the baseball glove he had mauled, and Chelsea of the party dress he puked on after eating the carton of brownies. Big mistake.

"Daddy," Susie cried, "my doll isn't real. Sammie is."

David shot back, "My baseball mitt can't get the ball for me, but Sammie always does."

Even grown-up Chelsea was hyperventilating. "Daddy, my date was a joke. Sammie loves me no matter what I'm wearing —and he'll love me forever."

Anticipating their reaction, Ruth began preparing the kids' favorite breakfast: blueberry buttermilk pancakes. We assembled around the table in sullen silence. Just as the first batch of pancakes was being passed around the table, Sammie trotted in.

He stopped, sniffed, and in one quick, smooth motion lifted his leg, twisted his body, and peed at least three and a half feet high on the kitchen wall.

That was it!

I didn't know I could bellow so forcefully. "Can you top that?"

A long, stiff silence.

David's soft voice finally broke the stillness. "Daddy, I'm not even going to try."

One more beat of silence until the five of us erupted into a communal belly laugh that could have been heard all the way to the pound.

We just celebrated Sammie's fifth adoption anniversary, and I'm convinced our family is closer than ever. I give a lot of the credit to a young man named David and a big black dog named Sammie.

—⎰ ⎱—

Children have the marvelous ability to see the humor in situations that annoy and upset adults. They also remind us, again and again, that if we just make a little extra effort, even the most ordinary experience can be transformed into something extraordinary and memorable.

Recently I attended the wedding of a good friend's daughter to a popular musician. The wedding was beautiful and inspiring. The reception featured the groom's band playing great dance music. Dads and daughters, mothers and sons, young couples, grandparents—everyone seemed to be enjoying themselves on the dance floor. My friend asked me to dance, but I was tired from a long, hard week. My feet hurt and my ears were ringing. I didn't even want to perform the custom-

ary brief dance with the bride. But as I began to catalog my
excuses for making a quick escape, my thoughts drifted to
the previous weekend.

Emmy, Ali, and I had enjoyed a mini-vacation at a bed
and breakfast mountain getaway. After a marathon Saturday
of hiking, shopping, baseball, and dinner, we staggered back
to our lodgings at half-past eight. Tired as they were, the
girls were still a little too excited to sleep. It was inquisitive
nine-year-old Ali who suggested we check out the game
room. I reluctantly agreed that they could head on over, and
I'd catch up in a moment. When I arrived less than five
minutes later, Ali was playing solitaire at the big table, and
Emmy was manipulating the handles on the popular soc-
cerlike Foosball table. Twelve-year-old Emmy was quick to
challenge me, and not more than two minutes into the first
game, I looked up to ask Ali to join us. She had already
fallen asleep on the table, blond hair spread out and cards
everywhere.

As Emmy and I continued our game, I struggled to keep
my eyes open and my attention focused. "I'll try to finish this
game," I muttered to Emmy, "but then we're going to have
to go to bed. I'm just too bushed."

She gave that a moment or two of thought, and then
with a coy grin on her face asked, "But, Daddy, isn't this why
we're here?"

Her simple statement stopped me cold. She was right, I
thought. That was exactly why we were here, to have fun. I
started to pay attention, and we both really got into the
game. Emmy named every member of her Foosball team,
giving them distinct personalities and even offering coaching
tips. I was captivated by her creativity and imagination, not
to mention her skill at the game.

Finally, I heard Emmy say, "Daddy, I'm really beat. Can

we go to bed now?" I did a double take on my watch. It was after eleven. I gathered up Ali and padded after Emmy down the hall to one of the most peaceful sleeps I can recall.

My friend said, "Come on, let's dance," and I was transported back to the wedding reception. I heard Emmy's words one more time. "Daddy, isn't this why we're here?" I smiled and accepted her invitation. And as we stepped out onto the floor, I wondered how many "dances" I had missed in the past.

CHAPTER FOUR

The Gift of Compassion

—⟆ ⟅—

A Helping Hand
Linda I. Brandt
Fort Benning, Georgia

Dog on a leash, baby in a stroller, toddler in tow—it was a beautiful autumn day in northern New York. Or was it? I was having a difficult time as the dog walked circles around the stroller until his leash became tangled in its wheels. Baby Tommy was fussing, and toddler Joey let go of my hand to walk ahead while I managed the mess we were in. I was feeling overwhelmed with how much trouble it was just to take a walk these days! When I bent over to care for Tommy (who was probably wondering why the three-ring circus stopped), the strap of my camera slipped off my shoulder and almost crashed on the ground.

Just then I looked up to check on Joey and noticed he was walking a few paces ahead with two women whom I did not recognize. Not only were they strangers, but Joey was holding the older woman's hand! After my initial stranger-alert terror had passed, I saw that the younger of the two women was helping her elderly mother take a walk down the street. Joey, completely on his own, had decided to help, too.

In that brief, tender moment I realized that my son would share my compassion for people with words unspoken. My heart stretched out to my little boy, and I felt fulfilled on a day when nothing seemed to be going right. After all, there's no greater gift we can receive from our children than one they give back.

For much of my life I have unwittingly stepped all over people in my frantic push for "success." Of all the lessons children have taught me, one of the most important is: We never walk alone. Our words and actions ripple out to help or hurt everyone around us. For children, compassion comes naturally. Caring for others is a gift of magnificent proportions if we are willing to follow our children's lead.

Love by the Armload
As told to LaVerna Braun, now Sister Barbara Ann, Lincoln, Nebraska, by her mother, Barbara Braun

To everyone in town my seventh child, my sweet little LaVerna, was known as "Grandma German's girl." She was always so good, so kind, especially to my mother. Mama, bless her soul, was severely crippled by arthritis. She managed to get around her small bungalow with the aid of two canes, but everything was difficult for her. Papa was very good to her, but as a retired farmer he loved to spend time in his large garden or playing cards with his friends in town at the pool hall. We lived only a block away in the small town of Humphrey, so LaVerna would visit her grandmother frequently and assist her any way she could.

Shortly after LaVerna started school, we moved about five blocks away, but she still went by every day to do errands. By the time she was eight we had decided that she should live with Mama and Papa German to be available whenever she was needed.

When LaVerna came home to visit us, I remember her telling me how much fun she had over there, although she worked hard. "I love baking sugar cookies," she said, "and I heed Grandma's warnings so I won't get burned." She helped Mama prepare meals, set and clear the table, dry dishes and put them away, dust and sweep the floors. When the work was done, she would sit at Mama's feet on a small stool and listen to her tales of pioneering days in Nebraska and Civil War days in Illinois.

Each week LaVerna gathered up their soiled clothes so I could wash them. Mama was so kind that she did the mending and darning for our big family in return. While LaVerna prepared her lessons in the evenings, I could picture my father reading the newspaper and my mother spending long hours in prayer. "Before we go to bed, we play a few games of 'fox and geese' or dominos," LaVerna told me. "And we listen to music or interesting records on the phonograph."

Mama always loved music, flowers, fine china, and crystal glasses. She would play tunes for LaVerna on the glasses with a spoon. LaVerna kept her many potted plants watered, and her grandfather repotted them as needed. Mama so enjoyed those plants in the big front window where she sat waving to all the passersby on Main Street.

My husband, Bill, received a promotion that would take our family to Omaha when LaVerna was just thirteen, a freshman in high school. It was such an agonizing decision for her. It was killing her, she said. She so dearly loved her grandparents, but the thought of the adventures of a big city was clearly calling her. And I know she didn't want to be so far away from her beloved brothers and sisters. Fortunately, my nephew was able to stay with Mama and Papa.

Oh, how sad moving day was. So many tears flowed. "I'll write and visit as often as I can," LaVerna kept saying to Mama and Papa. We did come back for weddings and funerals. Since Mama was unable to climb the stairs at church, dear LaVerna always remained with her during the church ceremonies. "It was just like old times," she said. "We counted the cars in the funeral procession as we did together for so many years."

And then, just a year and two months after we had left Humphrey, Mama became very ill from the flu and I had to return. "Please let me go with you," LaVerna begged over and over.

"No, child, you have to stay here and not miss classes," I told her firmly.

My heart broke twice while I watched as Mama lay dying, and I hadn't let my sweet daughter be there. I remember how often LaVerna told me that Mama would embrace her and press her to her heart, saying, "I love you more than anyone in the world, even more than my own children." They had taught each other the power of love.

Mama's only words as she left us were "LaVerna, LaVerna, LaVerna . . ."

Like so many parents, I have learned that children may not express their generosity the way I think they ought to.

The Empty Easter Basket
Karin Lamb
Kilmarnock, Virginia

It was a hot San Antonio Easter morning in 1963. I was a young Air Force bride from Germany just learning to adapt to American culture. My life centered around my two young girls, Pandora and Claudette, and today was special because their father was home from his tour of duty to celebrate Easter.

The girls were decked out in their frilly dresses, bonnets and all. We colored Easter eggs, and I had bought lots of candy, more than we could really afford, but after all, this was their first American Easter.

We had an Easter egg hunt, and when it was over, the girls' baskets were brimming. Several neighborhood children joined them in our front yard, and I was so proud of them both as I watched them playing and laughing with the others.

When they came back up the walk a short time later, I saw that Claudette's Easter basket, which had been brimming with chocolates, candy, jelly beans, and eggs just minutes before, was completely empty! How could she? I cried to myself. I had worked so hard to make it perfect, to buy more than we really could afford, and Claudette had given every single piece away!

I was so angry I bolted from the window to the door. Claudette came running up to me with blond curls flying and a huge smile on her face.

"Mommy, Mommy," she said. "I had so much fun. I gave all my candy to the Easter kids!"

I stopped in mid-breath. How could I be angry when she had just demonstrated warmth and generosity to the other children? How could I rob her of the joy she felt in giving? And I thought I knew what a perfect Easter should be!

The Largest Love from a Little Girl
Elizabeth C. Shoemake
Hattiesburg, Mississippi

I have always been proud that I came from a large family. Being the youngest of seven children always gave me a ready-made support group. But I never thought the emotional support I would receive when I needed it most would come from a six-year-old girl.

Anna weighed less than five pounds when she was born to

my sister Barbara. She was always a very petite child, but what she lacked in size she made up for in spunk and character. She was outspoken ever since she learned to talk before her first birthday. She loved teaching things to her little brother, Richard, and her younger cousins.

When Barbara had to go to Birmingham, Alabama, to have surgery to repair a defective heart valve, she expected to be home in ten days. That did not happen. Complications led to three more surgeries and several small strokes. She did not regain consciousness. But before her first operation she had asked that Anna and Richard not be allowed to see her until she was out of the intensive care unit. She knew she would be connected to a respirator, and she didn't want the tubes and machines to frighten them.

I can understand why. Seeing her even frightened me. There were tubes coming out of every part of her body, and she was connected to numerous machines including a heart pump that made a sickening clicking sound as it fluttered under the sheets.

Her body was so swollen that at first sight I was certain it was not my sister lying there. The swelling made her skin very dry and tight, and the strokes caused her hands to stay stiffly rolled in tight fists. It was difficult for the adults in my family to see her in that condition, and we were definitely apprehensive about the children's visiting her. But the truth was that if the children did not see her now, they might never see her again. She was very close to death.

Barbara was transferred to the heart transplant intensive care unit so that visitation would be easier. In no time the bulletin board in the room was covered with get well wishes from her family, friends, and the high school students to whom she was known as Mrs. B., their Spanish teacher. At the foot of her bed was the ever-present heart pump with all its switches and red lights, connected to her heart through tubes hidden by the sheets on the bed.

Anna had sewn together two scraps of fabric with crude stitches and stuffed it with tissue to make a small pillow for her mother. We put it in Barbara's fist to keep her fingernails from digging into her hands. On her bed there was a gift from Anna and Richard, a small stuffed animal on which we pinned holy medals, some bought at a nearby monastery and some sent to her by friends and family. In her left hand she clutched a rosary given to her by the hospital's priest on the first day of her surgery.

More surgeries followed, and the complications mounted. It seemed that Barbara would never recover. Finally, on Christmas Day, she began slowly to regain consciousness, but it was more than two weeks before she was coherent.

After that, some family member would take Anna to see her mother almost every weekend. She had to stand on a chair and stretch her whole body over the bed just to reach her mother's face. When Anna was wearing the required surgical mask, the only visible part of her face was her brown eyes, the same eyes as her mother's. Those eyes showed more expression than words could ever say. They asked questions, they laughed, and they poured love straight from the heart—but they never cried. Anna knew her mother wanted her to be strong, so tears did not flow from her eyes as long as she was in that room. In that room she kept her emotions hidden. Her mother's feelings were all that mattered to her.

As I watched Anna gently stroke her mother's hair and carefully lay her head on her chest, there were times when I had to go to the window or out of the room to hide my own tears. Knowing that her mother did not want to see her in the intensive care unit, Anna would reassure her, "It's going to be all right, Mama."

Before Barbara regained full consciousness, she would look up at Anna, terrified, but Anna continued to comfort her and tried to explain where she was and what was happening to her. She would hold her mother's hand and say soothingly, "Don't make that face, Mama. I'm not scared."

The mass of tubes did not faze Anna. She paid no attention to the constant jumping and clicking of the heart pump. It was then that I learned something very important from a child just six years on this earth: Compassion comes directly from the heart. Anna was blind to her mother's visible physical condition because she was feeling with her heart, not seeing with her eyes. Her courage was overwhelming. We all tried so hard to be strong for Anna's sake, but there was no need. She was the one who kept us strong. Her positive attitude and faith led us through the pain we all felt.

Barbara finally regained full consciousness on January 14, 1995, the day before her forty-second birthday. She was over-joyed to have her little girl with her, and she asked Anna to demonstrate her gymnastics skills by doing back flips and splits for the nurses and hospital staff. As usual, the nurses were charmed by Anna, and they let her get away with almost any-thing.

At the end of one visit, a nurse asked Anna if she would like to kiss her mother. She said yes, and for the first time she was allowed to take off her face mask. The nurse held her as she leaned over and kissed her mother on the lips.

That was the last time Anna saw her mother alive. She died on February 26. My sisters and I had planned to take Anna to Birmingham to be with her mother because we knew she had taken a turn for the worse. We didn't even know she had died until about five minutes before we planned to leave. We couldn't tell Anna; it was her father's place to break the news to her.

We drove to Birmingham, and the next day, after she had time to think about her mother's death, Anna asked us how Barbara was going to get home. She hoped the hospital would fly her body home because "my mama always loved to fly." Anna's main concern was not for herself but for her mother's welfare.

Facing a long four-hour drive home, we stopped at a gas station for the children to get a snack. I was sitting quietly in the front seat, thinking about my sister and hoping my sadness would not upset Anna. As she got out of the car she stopped and patted me on the shoulder, and in her calm, gentle voice she said, "I know just how you feel."

B efore my daughters were born, my journey through life always seemed to revolve around myself—acquiring things, getting ahead, being somebody. But the more I gained, the lonelier I got, and a big dark hole gaped in my life. Emmy and Ali have filled that hole with light, and of the many gifts my children have given me, perhaps the most important has been the reminder of the joy in caring for others.

My own daughters' fondest wish came true on Christmas Eve, 1991. Just before dark they ran in from playing in newly fallen snow to find me sitting next to the Christmas tree holding a seven-week-old black Labrador puppy. Amid squeals of delight and sparkling eyes, Emmy, then seven, Ali, five, and "Mister Wister" began a love affair that's still going strong.

Over the next several days we spent every waking hour playing with this wiggling, licking, tail-wagging bundle of puppy energy. We didn't tire of him until it was time to go to bed. Unfortunately, he didn't tire even then. We put his little wire kennel on the hall floor halfway between the girls' room and mine, and during the first few evenings I was up countless times shouting, "Stop that noise. Be quiet. Quit that." My dog training strategy seemed to work well—for about ten minutes.

On the third night I woke up to a different sound. Wister was doing his usual yipping and whining routine, but I also heard somebody singing. I crept out of bed and peeped out the door of my room. Little Ali was sitting on the floor beside the kennel singing the Dolly Parton song "Daddy's Hands." I became as lost as Wister appeared to be in her sweet voice and the beautiful words:

Daddy's hands were soft and kind when I was crying.
Daddy's hands were hard as steel when I'd done wrong.
Daddy's hands weren't always gentle, but I've come to
    *understand, there was always love in Daddy's hands.**

She sang the song through another time, reached in and stroked Wister's little head, whispered, "I love you," and went to bed. Wister slept through the night from then on. Clearly Ali's compassion and caring worked far better than my anger and shouting.

Gifts of No Return
Lori Regehr
Yorkton, Saskatchewan

I recall as a proud aunt taking my four- and seven-year-old nephews out for the evening some years back. We went to a little diner famous for its chips and hot dogs. When we had finished, Julian, the older of the two, took the fifty cents he'd been given by his parents for spending money and put it on the table as a tip. "Oh, no, you keep that," I said quickly. "I'll leave the tip."

Julian put the money back in his pocket, and we headed to the cash register where there was a large glass showcase filled with a tempting assortment of candies and gum. Right next to the cash register stood a little donation box for spare change. Julian spotted it immediately and read its inscription: PURPLE CROSS.

"What's that for?" he asked. I didn't know, so I looked to the cashier for help.

---

* ("Daddy's Hands," words and music by Holly Dunn. © 1986 EMI Blackwood Music Inc. All rights reserved; international copyright secured. Used by permission.)

"I'm not sure," she said, "but I think it's to fund medical research for helping children who can't hear."

"Can I put my money in there?" asked Julian, his eyes bright with anticipation.

"If you like," I said. Julian deposited his two quarters in the box. Not a word from either of the boys about wanting a treat. The cashier looked down at them in amazement. "How do you raise such incredible children?" she asked.

"I'm just their aunt," I said, marveling myself at their beautiful generosity.

After they were tucked away in bed at home that night, I told their mother what Julian had done. "The little box must have reminded them of last Christmas," she said with a smile.

She told me that through the Advent season she and my brother had decided to involve the boys in the spirit of giving. They placed a coin box under the Christmas tree along with the growing assortment of brightly wrapped packages and told the boys that whenever anyone in the family felt excited about Christmas, they could put something into the box. Then just before Christmas they would open the box and take the money as a family to buy a basket of treats for a family that couldn't afford a special Christmas. She said it was a lovely thing to see those boys stealing down the stairs most mornings to slip part of their allowance into that box before settling down to shake packages or just marvel at the beautifully decorated tree.

The memory of that incident in the diner and their mother's explanation continues to be a humbling reminder for me about giving without thought of return.

A Pacifier for the Weary
Beth Milam
Hattiesburg, Mississippi

Our daughter was frequently hospitalized with severe complications of diabetes, so my husband and I often took care of our granddaughter, Amy. At two and a half years old she was outgoing, active, full of fun, a good conversationalist, and mature for her age—with the exception of an inordinate addiction to her pacifier.

Amy was spending one hot Mississippi summer day with us. The heat, humidity, and Amy's spirits were all high, and we spent the morning at the park swinging, sliding, and feeding the animals, especially the rabbit we had donated to the park after it had outgrown our house.

After a picnic lunch of "sammiches and lemolade" and a short nap (for Amy), we spent the afternoon grocery shopping, making cookies, and playing games. My husband, a former coach, encouraged her athletic aptitude, so our ball games were vigorous, rambunctious, and exciting.

After such a long, strenuous, fun-filled day, Amy and I were both ready for an early bedtime. She kissed all her stuffed animals good night, said her lengthy bedtime prayers, and finally climbed into bed. Lying on the bed beside her, I read her three bedtime stories, and when she asked for a fourth, I breathed a huge sigh.

"Here, Nana," Amy said, detecting my weariness and patting me with her chubby little hand. "You can use my pacifier." She never asked for it again, at least not for the last eighteen years.

Life often seems like a jigsaw puzzle with several pieces missing. The gifts our children give us help us find those missing pieces. They help us evolve and grow. For too many years I carefully constructed a stronger-than-Kryptonite shield around my heart. It was very effective in keeping out the pain, but it kept love out, too. The compassion of children reminds me to let that shield down and genuinely care about others. Perhaps that's our most important calling. No responsibility is more crucial—whether with kids, friends, neighbors, or coworkers—than being constantly aware that how we listen or react or laugh or smile unfailingly touches those we care about, just as their words and actions touch us.

Not Enough Stephen to Go Around
Ann Brooks Francis
Midlothian, Virginia

It was the day of the fifth grade end-of-the-year picnic. Although the day dawned slightly overcast with the threat of rain, we decided to pretend the clouds wouldn't have the audacity to rain on our outing. Unfortunately, we were wrong, but the children persevered. It would certainly have taken more than a few raindrops to dampen the enthusiasm of these kids. After all, they were graduating from elementary school at the end of the week and moving on to the sophisticated world of middle school: lockers, homerooms, changing classes, and more.

Among the students in that class was a young man named Stephen, age thirteen, whom I did not know. Stephen was disabled. I later learned he had some type of seizure disorder and problems with balance. He was considered profoundly learning delayed, but with much success he had attended a special education program for most of his school career. The special ed program included as much "mainstreaming" as possible, and Stephen had participated with other students in the regular classroom when feasible. Now he was graduating.

"It was more a privilege than a chore for the students to work with Stephen," his mother had told me. "In every way they treated him as if he were one of their friends." Indeed, after watching a softball game on that rainy Monday in June, I had no doubt that Stephen was a very special friend of these young children. Although people unfamiliar with someone who is disabled might have found the situation disconcerting or uncomfortable, this was apparently not the case for these fifth graders.

His mother told me that Stephen's grandfather had visited the school one day and was amazed at what he observed. Stephen was in the regular classroom when he missed a chair and fell. The other kids paid little attention; they did not snicker or run to coddle and assist him. They knew Stephen was perfectly capable of recovering on his own, as would any other classmate. Sure enough, he righted himself, and his grandfather was witness to this simple acceptance of Stephen, just as he was, by this roomful of preadolescents.

Later, my son Scott revealed to me that while many children volunteered to read to Stephen or work with him, there "just wasn't enough Stephen to go around." At the school picnic I experienced firsthand the beauty of this unprejudiced acceptance of someone different from themselves. Or perhaps what I learned was that Stephen wasn't really so different after all. I wrote to the principal that afternoon to tell her what I had seen.

June 12, 1995
Dear Mrs. White:

   As the school year draws to a close and Evergreen's fifth graders prepare to move on to middle school, I wish to share an observation with you that I made while attending the fifth-grade picnic this morning with my son, Scott.

   The students split up into different groups to play soccer, kickball, take a hike, or play softball. I joined in to play softball with my son, and as I stood in right field (isn't that where they always put the rookie player?), I witnessed a maturity and kindness of spirit that I found remarkable in a large group of preadolescents.

A young man, Stephen, obviously handicapped, was helped out to the plate for a turn at bat. With a little help he made a hit, albeit not very hard, nor did it go very far. Without a word said among the dozen or so children, and as Stephen began his assisted run to first base, somehow the ball was bungled, then it was overthrown, then bungled again. The Bad News Bears would have looked like the Atlanta Braves next to the outfield's handling of this particular ball. And what do you know: Amid cheers of encouragement, Stephen made it to first base.

Play continued and somehow an out was made, but never at the base Stephen was heading for, even though that was often the obvious and easy play. Again, there was lots of good-natured bungling of the ball and words of encouragement for Stephen as he cleared first one base, then another, ending in a run for the batting team. Both teams cheered Stephen's score.

As a parent, my heart swelled with pride for these young people. Without a word to each other, and barely an exchanged look, they certainly made, in my humble opinion, the "right choice" in a world that is filled with wrong choices. As they move into middle school, may they continue to make this type of "right" choice.

Sincerely,

Ann Brooks Francis

And my thanks to Stephen for teaching his peers a lesson in life that can only make them into the kind of people we all aspire to be.

CHAPTER FIVE

The Gift of Letting Go

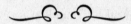

Not the Perfection of the Game
Anne Lazurko
Weyburn, Saskatchewan

I always marvel at the ability of children to say hilariously funny things, gems which, seconds later, kick you in the gut with their wisdom.

One day my four-year-old daughter, Sara, was watching professional golf on television (not a usual or particularly thrilling pastime). Struck by the ability of one player in particular, she observed, "Look, Mommy, that guy is really good. He didn't let that hole catch his ball."

After cracking up every time I thought about or repeated her remark, a new interpretation emerged. As adults we, too, often begin to see life as a slovenly and often futile attempt to play by rules dictated by some force outside ourselves. But the joy of a child is obviously not in the perfection of the game but in the perfection of what one perceives the game to be.

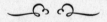

As parents we are so often caught up in the business of everyday life, trying to juggle a hundred things at once, that consciously or unconsciously control becomes a top priority. We make all the rules, and from the kids' perspective it seems as though we are trying to control everything and everybody. The result is that we blunt our senses and see everything in narrow, preconceived ways. We miss a lot of opportunities to do and see things differently, to just let ourselves go and enjoy life.

I was rushing around in a frenzy to get a package ready for a delivery service pickup by 4:30 P.M. It was clear that I wasn't going to make it even though I had driven everyone else in the office crazy trying to get it out.

Emmy was quietly watching all the commotion from her perch on the steps. "Is that the only delivery service there is, Daddy?" she asked.

Major slap-to-the-forehead time! Of course it wasn't. It was just the one we always used without questioning. A quick call found another service that gave us a two-hour reprieve.

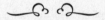

Children teach us that there's more than one way to do things. They love to experiment and try things out. They're not afraid to be open with their thoughts and feelings, and be spontaneous in their actions. For years I thought there was only one way to do things—the way that had worked before or the way that was my habit or the way other people said it had to be done. I now see that children embrace a different philosophy. In their world they see a fascinating variety of options and choices. And when I can look at the world from their point of view, I can let go of old patterns and habits and find a lot more options than I had ever dreamed possible.

No Longer One Path
Corene Walsh
Ann Arbor, Michigan

Casey wakes up; we know what is ahead for both of us. I speak first about the day. Casey begins to cry. "I'm afraid, Mommy."

"It's okay, Casey," I say. "It's okay to be afraid. You are growing up, and all big boys have to do this someday."

"Mommy, I don't want to grow up."

"But the world is waiting for such a special boy like you," I reassure him. "We'll do this together, Casey. I promise."

While I get dressed, I feel the fear well up inside. I'm afraid he might need me and I won't be there. In the car: I see a red nose and red eyes in the rearview mirror. I reach back my hand —I could hold his little hand forever. What if I can't leave him? What if I'm not strong enough to let go? What if I cry?

We pull up to the school and walk slowly inside. "I don't want to go, Mommy. What if I need you? You won't be there. What if I cry?"

We sit awhile in the classroom, but it's time for me to go. Can I do this? I look into his little blue eyes filled with tears. I have to say good-bye. "I love you, Casey." I hug him. He holds on. I hug more, and he holds on more. I let go, choking on my words. "You will do great today, I know you will," I say. "Have a good day."

I step out the door and walk down the hall wiping away tears. What if he comes after me? I turn and he is there.

"Mommy, don't leave me. I'm so scared." I want to protect him! I want him to feel safe! I want to help him to be strong! I will have to send him back in. . . . I sit with him for a while, then kiss him good-bye. I leave quickly. I feel awful inside. How can I do that to him?

How couldn't I? That morning goes by slowly. Finally it is time to pick him up. I am excited. I want to hug him and tell him I was strong. I let him go. I came back for him, and he was there.

He sees me, smiles, and hugs me. He tells me he was strong, and he didn't run after me. He let me go, and I came back for him. "I love you, Mommy."

"I love you, too, Casey."

That first day of kindergarten will live in my memory forever. It was the end of my being Casey's whole world and the beginning of a new world for Casey. New people will come into his life who will help mold him into a good man someday. The path we walk together is no longer one path. It is two paths alongside each other.

Even though it's hard for me to walk along different paths from my children, I know it's important that I do so. One of the most meaningful lessons I've learned from them is that while they invite me to enter and enjoy their world, they draw the line when I try to dictate their lives. We can walk in the same direction, but as they have grown older, more and more often the path is one of their own choosing.

Of course, along the way, I'm scared to death for them. What if they make mistakes? I know how they could get an A on that school project, but it's their homework. Or what if they get hurt? I'm certainly not going to let them run in front of a speeding car. Although I will always give my daughters clear guidelines when it comes to dangerous or moral situations, they have clearly shown me over and over again that I can't live their lives for them. And when I do so, I stunt their growth—exactly the opposite of what I'm trying to do. We evolve and grow until the day we die, and my children are teaching me to step back and honor that process.

I remember how I agonized over a little pair of red cowboy boots. They weren't even my boots; they were five-year-old Ali's most prized possession. She adored those boots. She polished them religiously, kept them dry and in their proper place. When she wore them, there was an extra jauntiness in her walk, a special sparkle in her smile. This was one little girl who knew how to step out in style!

Suddenly, however, long before she outgrew them, Ali was ready to move on. She no longer had any interest in those boots. But while she simply left them behind, I went through all sorts of turmoil about how she was growing up too quickly. She embraced change while I fought it like an unyielding stone. But gradually I've come to understand that growth and change are not only inevitable, they are also necessary all through both the painful and joyful business of growing up.

There in the midst of tutus and ballet slippers and fanfare, I think I was more nervous than either of my three- and five-year-old daughters at their first dance recital. But when the performance was over, I felt nothing but overwhelming pride and love as I gave them congratulation bouquets. And at every performance since, when the final curtain falls, I've waited in the audience with two bouquets of flowers. After exchanging hugs and kisses, thank-you's and I-love-you's, all three of us would go out for a special dinner.

Then in the fall of 1995, when Emmy was twelve and Ali was ten, both girls had excellent parts in *The Wizard of Oz*. After the opening night performance, I was waiting as usual in the audience with my two bouquets of flowers. A flushed, excited Ali looked for me immediately and rushed over for a big hug. I congratulated her as I presented her with her bouquet.

But Emmy was different this time. She couldn't seem to

find me in the crowd. I didn't understand what was going on. I was standing in plain sight, waving at her, calling her name, but she was looking in every direction but mine. Then I got it. She wasn't looking for me, she was looking for her friends. Finally, she came down from the stage, but all she said was "Hi, Dad."

Was this my daughter, I wondered? What had happened to the hugs and kisses and "I love my flowers!"

Emmy finally gave me a quick hug and took her flowers. Then she grabbed my arm and pulled me toward the exit. At least she still wants to go out for dinner, I thought. "Come on, Dad, we're going to be late," she said, pulling a sweater on over her tights. "Can't you go any faster?"

I was confused. "Late for what?" I asked.

"The party," Emmy said. "Come on, it started ten minutes ago."

In my excitement I'd forgotten all about it. So Ali and I dropped Emmy off at the party, and we were just a twosome for our traditional dinner. I tried hard to be fully present for Ali, but I have to admit I had a hard time concentrating on dinner. I squeezed back my tears until Ali went to bed and Emmy came home from the party.

Were they tears of sadness? Not completely. Was it fear or concern? Not really. Was it pride? Partly. Was it the process of letting go? Mostly.

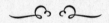

The baby steps Emmy had taken years ago were much easier, I realized. I had celebrated when she learned to pour her own milk. I was thrilled when she could walk to school by herself. But now she was teaching me to look forward to the big steps, too, and even welcome them.

When we trust and honor the process of their growth and change, there is little need for our children to resist and rebel. But if we slip into a clutching, control-and-criticize mode, all hell can break loose. Kids know instinctively when they are ready for the next step. The question is, are we willing to let them take it?

Shouting Matches
Richard Suwanski
Elmwood Park, Illinois

Our third-born child is different—very independent, street smart, and someone who challenges everything. Given these characteristics, he and I had many heated discussions. One day while I was driving him somewhere, we started shouting at each other again. I looked over at him in disgust and said, "Why are we wasting time even talking to each other?"

After a moment of silence he replied, "Because you're my dad!"

I was both humbled and unhappy. I realized that even though he was fifteen years old and six feet tall, I had been relating to him as an adult or business colleague. I had forgotten who he was—my son. But he hadn't forgotten who I was—his dad. He still needed input and direction. That lesson didn't immediately end all the loud discussions, but it sure changed how we related to each other.

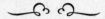

Letting go does not mean letting our kids walk all over us. Just as much as they don't want us to dictate and lecture and control them, they also don't want namby-pamby parents who don't even care enough to give them guidelines.

I've learned that we can let go by default or by choice.

Letting go by default, usually out of sheer frustration, means not knowing what our children are doing or just telling them what not to do and then throwing our hands up when they do the opposite. Letting go by choice means that we are fully aware of the choices our children are making and give them the guidelines that will enable them to make the right choices. Of course, there will still be times when we have to say, "No, I don't believe you're quite ready for that yet," and then explain why and mutually explore other options.

When our children have learned to think for themselves and have routinely been honored and trusted for their thoughts and decisions, they usually respect us when we have to say no. They know that we are paying attention and want the very best for them. In both subtle and obvious ways, our kids teach us when and how to let go. Even so, it can be a very difficult lesson to learn.

Gold or Gloom?
Alice H.
Denver, Colorado

What a glorious Rocky Mountain day! Dazzling sunshine, light mountain breezes, a sky so blue, God must have invented the color just for this moment. I'd been housebound all winter and most of the drizzly damp spring, and this was heaven-on-a-trail as we hiked through mind-boggling canyon rocks along a still-full mountain creek.

My neighbors had not hesitated at all to ask me along on their outing, even though my recuperation from back surgery did not allow me to walk far or to carry anything but the basics: jacket, water, snacks.

No problem, they had assured me. They kept their hikes short and easy in order to accommodate the youngest children, and the older ones could easily fit extra food and equipment for our picnic lunch into their own backpacks. I didn't have to bring a camera along. They'd get extra film for theirs to take pictures that I wanted—especially the one of me back in the outdoors so I could show my family I was doing fine.

Hiking in the high country is always a study in contrasts, but today the differences that stuck in my mind were not in nature itself but in the nature of families. Standing in the same spot on the trail, I observed two vastly different scenarios unfold.

One series of comments went like this: "Where did you get that slimy rock? Watch out, it's dripping all over your shirt. I don't care if you think it has gold in it, put it down before your brother tries to put it in his mouth. And don't go down to the water again unless I'm holding on to you."

The other unfolded like this: "Hey, I noticed you down by the creek. Thanks for remembering to test the sand before stepping near the water and to keep your buddy nearby. What did you find? Gold? Wow, let's look at that. Remind me of the things that differentiate gold from other minerals. Should we take this along to look it up in that book at home?"

Later on: "Watch out on those rocks. You know how many people die rock climbing every year? And snakes. You know they hide in the shadows this time of day. Don't put your fingers in your mouth. You've probably touched something poisonous. I don't care if you're hungry. We'll all eat together when it's time."

And from the other family: "Nice work climbing those rocks. It looked as if you remembered everything we discussed about safety. Your little sister is ecstatic—she loves to follow you and listen to all your explanations. And you even had those fancy Band-Aids in your backpack for her scraped knee. Mine are plain old tan. Hungry? What snacks do you have in your pack to tide you over until we get to the picnic grounds?"

I know it wasn't the result of just this one encounter, but, here's what I saw by the end of our walk. Family Number One: Children afraid of everything, constant whining and complaining, siblings bickering, very low self-esteem, children constantly getting hurt, Mom with a massive headache, lots of complaining about how much hassle children are, and no enjoyment in being together.

Family Number Two: Fun, love, joy, learning together, appreciation of one another and the outdoors, high self-esteem, children believing in themselves, supporting each other, falling down and moving on to the next activity, family members who truly seemed to enjoy being together.

As much as I appreciated both families' sincere desire to include me in their activities, I think I'll be pretty selective in whose invitation I accept next time.

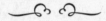

Families that deprive their kids of their independence deprive themselves of the opportunity to learn and grow right along with them. By teaching each other, both children and adults can learn and evolve at warp speed. Children give us a chance to get life right.

You Win, I Lose
(From an anonymous teacher)

It had been a very long year, and I was thankful that we were just two weeks away from summer break. I and all twenty-six of my first graders were more than anxious to escape. But now, in the middle of May, we were having a record heat spell, the air-conditioning was out in our portion of the building, and we were all nearing our boiling point.

And then there was the issue of Johnny Tucker. Frankly, one reason I was anxious for summer was that I could pass Johnny on to one of my colleagues in the second grade. Johnny wasn't dumb; in fact, his grades were slightly above average. It's just that he was always causing me extra work and extra headaches. One day it would be a squabble or fight, the next day a spilled can of glue or paint. And if he couldn't mess up the obvious, he would find a whole new way to create mischief and disruption.

His list of infractions was long and getting longer. For example, he was certainly smart enough so that he didn't need to cheat. It just seemed to be more fun or maybe the only thing he knew. I sometimes wondered if he did it just to bug me. And even if he wasn't cheating, he would always try to whisper back and forth even though there was no talking during test time.

As I released the children for their twenty-minute afternoon recess on that scorching Friday afternoon, I stayed a few steps behind and kept my eye on Johnny. He had been disruptive with the children and me all day, and I was expecting more of the same. In a split second after he hit Nathan, I had Johnny by the arm up against the building. At my wits' end, I shouted, "Why did you hit Nathan?"

Johnny didn't struggle. He just stood quietly for a moment before he said, "I don't know what to tell you. If I lie, I'll get in trouble, and if I tell the truth, I'll get in trouble."

I don't know if I would have gotten the message on a more sane and calm day, but that day his words reached out and grabbed me harder than any single moment in my fifteen-year teaching career. I asked my aide to watch my students, and I went inside the building and stumbled down the hall, through the teachers' lounge, and into the little supply room on the far side. I sat on a box in the corner for a long time. Johnny's words had said it all. He couldn't win because I was always looking for him to be bad.

By the time I returned to my class I had decided it wasn't too late to make a mid-career course correction. My job wasn't at stake, but my children were. It would be just as easy to help make the little Johnnies of the world believe they were good as to help them believe they were bad.

That was fourteen years ago, and ever since that hot May day when I begin to notice that a child is weak at pronunciation, slow at reading, poor at listening, sloppy at lettering, or disruptive in class, I've learned that my number one job is to discipline myself to look for just the opposite. Does it work perfectly? No. But in my opinion the difference is life-changing.

As for Johnny Tucker, I kept an eye on him for years. It was never easy for him, but he made it. I will always be convinced that if I had made a conscious choice to look for just the opposite of the rotten stuff I was so certain he would do, we all would have achieved more—Johnny, the other kids, their parents, and, of course, myself. To this day it still surprises me that it wasn't my framed master's degree that taught me how to really make a difference. It was a six-year-old boy named Johnny.

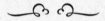

The best teachers know that "children are meant to be unfolded, not molded" and that we have to step back to let kids go and to let them grow. Perhaps the best way to let go is described by this anonymous poet.

Let me know when I make you proud.
And help me to have pride in my own accomplishments.

Let me earn your trust. Then trust me.
I won't let you down.

Let me try my wings. If I fail, let me know it's okay.
And encourage me to try again.

Let me know you love me. With a hug. Or a pat on the back.
    Or, when I need it,
With a firm but gentle "no."

Let me be. Let me change. Let me grow.

Let me tell you when I'm feeling bad. Or angry. Even at you.
And let me know that even on my worst days, you still like me.

Let me dream. Share my joy when my dreams come true.
Share my tears when they don't.

Let me feel secure in my home. Help me realize that love is
*   always there;*
that I can depend on you no matter what.

Let me run . . . let me laugh . . . let me play.

And most of all, let me be a child.

CHAPTER SIX

The Gift of Learning

—⟨₃ ₂⟩—

Dear Santa

May I please have a few wish worlds sets? and a
keyboard one one that & plays by itself and bring me
whatever you want

Love Emily to Santa

Emmy's letter reminded me that "The dog went to the barn" was probably the most exciting sentence I ever wrote at her age because I was so concerned about having the words right instead of writing about what truly interested me. Our children teach us that it's okay to make mistakes because they challenge us to move forward. Certainly I want my children to spell and use grammar correctly, but I'm proud that they do not let spelling problems stand in the way of creativity.

Emmy gave me another little gem of wisdom, too: In order to tap into the abundance of life with all its ideas and opportunities, it doesn't hurt to ask for a "fourth wish."

Because most of us are reluctant to learn anything new, we are condemned to keep doing things the same old way. Our children can teach us how to become lifelong learners in their marvelous classroom. They help us keep a questing attitude and remind us that learning from mistakes is a journey of honor and greatness instead of stupidity and slowness.

They also remind us that life is an ongoing process of learning and evolving, asking questions, seeking, growing. They give us an opportunity to step out of the limiting boxes of old patterns and belief systems and see the world afresh each day—or maybe just a closet door.

The girls had asked me if I could fix one of their accordion-style closet doors. So with a little bit of spare time and toolbox in hand, I checked it out. The right-hand door was totally stuck. Using my screwdriver like a doctor's scalpel, I began to analyze the problem. This should take just a minute, I thought. But five minutes later, both the door and I were stuck. I just couldn't figure out what in the world was wrong with that door.

"Daddy, let's look at it from over here," Emmy called from her bed where she'd been watching me from across the room.

"What?" I said, still frowning.

"Let's look at it from over here," she repeated.

Just to let her know I was really listening, I muttered, "Okay" and walked over to her bed.

We both stared in silence for a few minutes, then pointed and exclaimed at the same moment. From that new perspective we could see that the door must have slipped off its track and was now mounted at a slight slant, keeping it wedged in the closed position. It took a short minute to adjust the appropriate mechanism and, presto, the door worked perfectly.

Back Off My Backside
Karen Smith
Freeport, Illinois

When my daughter was eighteen months old, she began to show an interest in the toilet. I was elated. I thought potty training was going to be a snap. At age three, however, she still wasn't potty trained.

Every day brought another yelling match. Finally, one day she screamed in exasperation, "I don't have to be potty trained at home. I am trained at the sitter's."

She was absolutely right, I thought. She never had an accident at the sitter's. What we had here was a textbook power struggle. But instead of screaming back at her, I said quietly, "From now on, sitting on the potty is completely your decision, and you'll do it when you're ready."

After three days she was completely potty trained!

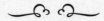

Everyone has to learn at his own pace. But my daughter Ali showed me recently that pace is not only a matter of *when* we're ready to learn but also *how long* we'll keep trying to learn.

Ali and I were standing at the door to our upstairs deck enjoying the beautiful day and the cool breeze. "Wow, look at that beautiful orange poppy," I said just as Emmy came into the room to see if we wanted to play cards.

Ten minutes into our game, Ali still hadn't joined us. I could see her standing at the door to the deck. "Ali, what are you doing? Don't you want to play cards?"

"Where is it, Daddy? I can't find it."

"What are you looking for, sweetie?"

"The puppy, Daddy. You said there was an orange puppy."

Sometimes my learning curve soars, sometimes it dives; often it stays stuck seemingly forever on a plateau. But the only way off a plateau is to stick with the task at hand. Ali was perfectly willing to believe I had seen an orange puppy, and she would see it, too, if she looked long enough.

Is Winning Everything?
Johnnie Farmer
Molina, Colorado

My oldest daughter has always had a passion for horses. Maybe it was because she rode with me in a backpack until she could sit in front of me and "guide" my horse.

As soon as she was big enough to ride alone, she started entering horse shows. I learned early on that to some horse show mothers winning was all that mattered. I saw them rant and rave and lecture their kids on their mistakes until the poor kids were so upset that it was a wonder they didn't shake right out of their saddles with the fear of what they'd have to face if they didn't win.

No way was I going to do that to my daughter! Of course, winning was important. After all, that's why she was there. But I decided to let her make up her own mind as to how important winning was while I tried to offer support in her endeavors without pushing.

Day after day she would ride that horse, either practicing an old maneuver or trying to learn a new one. She never seemed to tire or lose interest. She was very good, and a lot of the time she would come out of that arena with a ribbon. Often it would be the blue ribbon.

But sometimes she or the horse would make a mistake, and they wouldn't be in the ribbons. I never saw her angry or discouraged. She'd ride out of that arena all wiggly, and her blue eyes would sparkle with excitement because she and her horse had done well on something they'd been working on. As for her mistake, well, she'd just have to work harder on that for next time.

I watched year after year as she developed the self-confidence to try. I saw her pride in her accomplishments, even the small ones.

Is winning important to her? You bet it is! It's just that she knows that earning a blue ribbon is not all that matters.

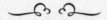

Maybe what allows learning to really flourish is that we don't always have to *be* the best but simply to *do* our best. Maybe having to be the best, to always be number one actually stifles learning and growth.

I was starting to feel pretty bad for Emmy and her basketball team last fall. Her fifth-grade team had a discouraging record of 0–6, and the margins were not pretty. They usually lost by thirty or forty points. It didn't take a Ph.D. to see why, either. Compared with most of the other teams, Emmy's team was smaller, slower, and less experienced. I thought she should be quite discouraged by now, too, but she seemed to love every practice and every game, and her teammates were enjoying them just as much.

"Emmy, how can you all be so excited about your team when you keep losing game after game?" I finally asked her.

Her answer stopped me short. "Oh, Daddy, we win almost every game. Our goal is to reach twelve points and to keep the other team under fifty. Our team is all fifth graders, and the other teams are mostly sixth graders. We think we're doing great!"

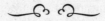

Who says we have to live by somebody else's rating system? Can't we decide how we're going to keep score? Can't we decide to see ourselves as a success instead of a failure? We can kill our ability to learn by getting into a comparison-based mentality where we're never good enough. It doesn't seem worth trying because someone else is always better.

Emmy's remark taught me an even more significant lesson. The most important thing that affects our self-image is living every moment knowing that we're doing our very best, although we may not be winning every game and every challenge.

In fact, Emmy and her team greatly improved that season, and they always had plenty of old-fashioned team spirit. I wonder how much they would have improved if they had been focused on how bad they were. What if these kids had put all their energy into blaming and judging?

So often children accept a situation just as it is and then make a treasure hunt out of learning the lessons that come along. What if we could bring the same kind of wisdom to our relationship with our kids? What if we could learn to accept and enjoy the circumstances of our kids' lives as they are instead of wishing they were some other way?

The Traveling Doll
Ila Bishop
Denver, Colorado

During the 1960s, when our two children were small, we lived in Pakistan where my husband worked as an engineer on a large irrigation project. In 1965, India and Pakistan went to war, and we were caught in the middle. On the first day, the U.S. government told us they would evacuate all Americans the next day. However, India and Pakistan took about ten days to decide when and how long they would cease firing in order for American planes to land.

While we waited for the fighting to stop, I spent my time packing and repacking the one suitcase I would be allowed to take out. This was quite a task because we were told to expect that we would never again see anything that was left behind. I also asked each of the children to pack a flight bag with their nightclothes, toothbrush, a change of clothes, and whatever toys they wanted to take. They were used to this since we traveled a great deal, and this was their standard packing procedure.

Bud, age six, packed his bag as usual. Cindy, age four, asked if she could take a doll. I said, "Of course." However, when it came time for me to give my okay on her flight bag, I was amazed to find it was filled with clothes for her biggest doll—one that was almost as tall as she was. I tried to explain that I was thinking of her Barbie doll, but Cindy held me to my promise and said she would carry the doll and the flight bag the entire trip with no help. I told her that she had to have clothes for herself and that the toys in the flight bag should be things that she and Bud could both play with or books that could be shared. No clothes were to be packed for the big doll.

The next time I checked, her flight bag was packed as I had asked, so all seemed to have been settled. Little did I know!

The American community was tense and on edge during the ten days we waited for evacuation. It soon became apparent that no men would be allowed to leave, only women and children.

This put an additional strain on all of us because we didn't know if we'd ever see our husbands and fathers again. No one slept much.

When we finally climbed wearily on board the U.S. Air Force C-131, we found four long benches the length of the plane, with seatbelts hanging from overhead racks. There were over one hundred women and children on the plane, and seatbelts for only about forty paratroopers. I put Cindy on my lap and pulled Bud close to me, then wrapped a belt around all three of us. The doll, to Cindy's disgust, did not get included.

As we took off, I had my hand on the doll and began to realize it didn't feel quite right. Sure enough, the doll was wearing its entire wardrobe, layered. Cindy explained that I had said she couldn't pack the clothes. It had taken her days to lay them out and dress and undress the doll until she had the smaller outfits on first and the looser ones on top. She certainly understood early that if you can't reach your goal one way, try another approach. And just as she had promised, she carried the doll and the flight bag halfway around the world without once asking for help. After that trip, whenever one of us in the family thought we had reached a dead end, someone would pipe up, "Find a way —dress the doll!"

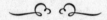

When it comes to solving problems, children seem to know intuitively that it is a simple two-step process. As a first step we have to accept what is, then we have to take responsibility for the next step. There's always a way to solve a problem instead of getting trapped in a cycle of whining about why it can't be done or why it's someone else's fault.

I think the most debilitating words in our language are "hopeless" and "impossible." As soon as we use those labels to describe a situation, sure enough that situation *is* either hopeless or impossible, and we are stuck. But when we accept what is and take responsibility for the next step, we can't ever be stuck. We may not know what the third or fourth step will be, but we can take the next small step and then find out what might be next.

Ask any five-year-old, "Can you draw? Can you sing? Can you dance?" and watch as they begin to draw with abandon, sing enthusiastically, and dance with verve and style. Ask any teenager the same questions—and then stand there waiting while they look at you like some sort of alien life form. When do we lose that desire to try and try again, grow and learn? Maybe there's a hint in this story a friend told me.

What's That Yucky Bug?

Nine bright-eyed, eager children squatted beside the wide bucket of water the camp counselor deposited on the sandy bank of the creek.

"Eeeewww, what is that yucky bug?" one squealed, pointing at the bucket.

"Cool," three others said nearly in unison.

"Why does it look so funny?" asked a little pigtailed girl, poking a tentative finger into the water.

"Look at those weird feet," shouted another.

"How can it swim like that?"

"Why doesn't it sink?"

"Will it bite?"

Questions flew out of their mouths almost as fast as the insect skittered across the water.

Great, I thought. These kids are very eager to learn. I could barely scribble notes in my reporter's pad fast enough to keep up with them. Thank goodness the cameraman was getting all this on tape. I hunkered down beside the kids to watch the learning process unfold.

"This water insect," the counselor began, "is a . . . Its

feet are like this because . . . It lives . . . reproduces . . . dies . . . eats . . . won't bite you . . ." On and on and on. She certainly knew her stuff, but the kids wouldn't remember any of it when she was done maybe ten minutes later. It seemed like an hour to me.

I watched their sparkling eyes glaze over, mouths snap shut on unasked questions, and their attention diverted to drawing their names in the sand with long sticks or feigning insect attacks on one another. I nearly dozed off in boredom myself. The picture of my seventh grade science teacher, Miss Oliver, kept flashing before my sagging eyeballs. She had been great at this, too: talk, lecture, tell—endlessly.

This was *not* going to be an easy feature to write in time for the ten o'clock news, I thought. I looked around for my cameraman. He was moving almost as fast as the water bug, camera swiveling from one busy, involved child to another in a group that had formed about fifty feet away. The group leader must not have started talking yet, I thought sarcastically; these kids are still reacting to the bugs in their bucket —questions, touching the water, more questions.

I edged closer. Same questions, much different answers.

"Why do their feet look like that?"

"What do you think?" Dan the counselor asked. (Thank goodness for big name tags.)

"I dunno." (Ah, I thought, I remember that answer!)

"How would you describe those feet?" Dan quizzed.

"Big." "Huge." Answers tumbled out. "Canoe paddles." "Clown shoes, ha, ha, ha."

"Where do these guys live?" Dan shot back. "What do they eat? . . . What tries to eat them? . . . Would these legs and feet help them swim faster to get away? . . . To grab their own food? . . . What do you think?"

The "dunnos" quickly changed to "maybe they . . ."

"what if . . ." "then they could . . ." And I think "signaling space aliens" slipped in there somewhere, too. But after the giggles stopped, the ideas kept flowing—out of the kids. Dan threw in a few hints when they were genuinely stuck, but I was amazed at how much five- and six-year-olds could figure out when the right questions were thrown their way.

This was going to be a heck of a story for the ten o'clock news.

CHAPTER SEVEN

The Gift of Listening

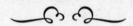

Deaf to Dumbo
Natalie Cruickshank
Princeton, New Jersey

My husband and I raised three wonderful children. During that time we shared love, pride in their accomplishments, frustration, heartache, and, finally, the realization that each would be a survivor in this world despite what we felt were many child-rearing mistakes. I did not expect to receive the greatest "life lesson" from our six-year-old granddaughter, Jessica.

On a sunny July day, "Grandpa," "Grammy," and Jessica traveled to a Point Pleasant, New Jersey, amusement park, featuring rides designed for the younger set. Jessica excitedly pointed to her "dream ride," an elephant carousel of brightly colored "Dumbos" gently rising and falling in the air to the sound of Disney tunes. We purchased twelve tickets and suggested to Jessica that she look at all the rides first since some required more tickets than others. There's a good math lesson to be learned here, I thought!

Jessica impatiently dashed along the boardwalk, quickly glancing at each ride but always glancing back to catch a glimpse of the "Dumbo" carousel. Soon she was happily sitting in a bright pink "Dumbo," flying through the air with an expression of sheer delight on her face. When the ride ended, I asked her which ride she would like next.

"Dumbo," she replied.

"But Jessica," I said, "there are so many others!"

Jessica hesitated a moment but then quietly agreed to a number of other rides, which I now realize she felt pressured to select. Before each ride she always asked how many tickets were left, and pretty soon all the tickets were gone.

"No more tickets for more rides," I said. "It's time to go home."

Jessica was very quiet when we got into the car. "What was your favorite ride?" I asked her.

She lowered her eyes and softly answered, "Dumbo, Grammy. I wished I could have ridden it all day."

I learned a very painful lesson at that moment. I had asked Jessica to make a choice. She had. And when she did, I hadn't listened. I was convinced in my "adult wisdom" that her park experiences would be enriched by additional rides.

I can't make up for the past—not truly listening over the years to what my own children had really meant despite what they said. I had heard only what I wanted or expected to hear. But I can make today and all our tomorrows so much better.

If there's one lesson that children teach us with abundant grace and wisdom, it is to learn how to listen, especially to the meaning and not just the words. Listening with awe and honor to what another person is saying, particularly our kids, lets us start to understand and value the essence of children and everyone around us. But sometimes that seems hard to do because we have already made up our minds. We know what we want to hear and where we want the conversation to go. And even though we don't always listen well, I've noticed that children sure do.

The Great Imitators
Michelle Williams-Grant
Newport News, Virginia

"Michael, you are now two years old today, you are potty trained, putting on your own clothes, and you are a big boy now, and I am berry proud of you."

I smiled as these words flowed from my three-year-old son Geoffrey to his little brother. I had said something similar to him on his second birthday, nineteen months before. But I was surprised because I didn't think that he was listening to me at the time or would even remember my "birthday speech" about how proud I was of him and the things that he had accomplished.

What a gift Geoffrey's words were. I realize now how much children imitate others, especially the adults in their lives. Our children are such special, precious gifts that we must always be aware of our awesome responsibility to be a positive focus in their lives.

I believe our children's essence, the very core of who they are, is like a fragile flame. All too often when we don't listen or when we focus on actions rather than on intentions, we can either snuff out that flame entirely or create a conflagration as kids resist and rebel against our heavy-handedness.

Who Can I Be if You Don't Listen to Me?
Sandra Bitner
Whitmore Lake, Michigan

My daughter, Lisa, showed defiance of authority at an early age, but underneath a hard shell was a soft heart. Her devil-may-care attitude caused her to run head-on into a teacher who saw in her a challenge. Failure to have homework done or to keep her desk clean or to achieve the expected grade was met with swift reprisal in this teacher's classroom.

When reprimanded, Lisa had a tendency to hide her true vulnerability and hurt feelings by bristling and fighting back like a cornered animal. She let no one see her cry, believing tears to be a sign of weakness. This, of course, was seen by her teacher as a further challenge. So began a year of punishment, defiance, more punishment, more defiance.

Lisa would come home obnoxious, belligerent, and ornery. My reaction, of course, was to punish her disobedience. Unaware of what was taking place at school, I saw only the misbehavior at home and could not allow this orneriness to go unpunished. My reaction only compounded the problem.

Finally, I noticed a pattern. When Lisa was "attacked" and humiliated by her teacher, her defense mechanism went into action, presenting an appearance of defiance and belligerence. This resulted in even harsher action by the teacher, and she would then come home with a bad attitude. I soon learned that her after-school attitude was in direct proportion to the severity of the run-in she had had at school with her teacher. Her behavior was not only a cover-up for bruised feelings, but she was crying out to me for reassurance that at home she was loved and accepted. We had to sit down together after school and talk about her day.

Parent-teacher-principal conferences brought no relief. I was a mere mother, and they were trained professionals. The idea of correcting a child in private or allowing her to receive a C when she was capable of an A was unacceptable to them. My plea for them to "back off" fell on deaf ears.

As a last resort I asked these professionals for a list of child counselors, which they rushed to provide. I promptly threw it away, but they thought Lisa was going for counseling. From that time on they "backed off," lifting the pressure. Lisa was even given little teacher's helper duties. Her attitude gradually improved, her grades rose, and her disposition after school was sunny. The rest of her school years were relatively uneventful.

Lisa is now a college sophomore studying elementary education and early childhood development. Her goal is to be a good teacher who listens to her students. She taught me not to accept people's actions alone but to look deeper for the causes. Those crabby customers or unpleasant coworkers aren't that way by choice. Something in their busy day or life has caused their unpleasantness. Perhaps they, like Lisa, are crying out for someone to listen and understand.

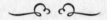

When parents really listen to their children, a bond is established between them that goes far beyond mere words.

My worst nightmare was coming true. After we had lived in the same town for years, which allowed for easy sharing of Emmy and Ali, my former wife announced that she and our girls were moving three hours away. She had just gotten engaged and was moving to her fiancé's hometown. I was happy for her engagement but depressed about my girls being so far away.

The warnings from my more experienced divorced friends were immediate and firm. "It's okay now that your daughters are seven and nine, but this move is going to cause you tremendous heartache when they're ten, eleven, twelve, and older. They're not going to want to be with you very much. At that age you have to be part of their chauffeur system and be involved with their activities and friends and lessons."

Another friend advised, "Without all of the things that

are so important to girls that age—friends, activities, and boys—you're going to have to create some 'bait' to hook them into time with you. Have you thought about a motorboat or a cabin by a lake?"

My friends were right. Within two years my daughters were involved in dance, basketball, tennis, numerous school activities, and a tight circle of friends in their new town. I couldn't blame them, but missing weekends with them made a deep dent in my heart.

My friends were relentless. "Get used to it, it's only going to get worse," they kept reminding me. Then about a year ago I attended a conference of educators and parents, and during one lively discussion a participant mentioned that her goal was to practice "heart listening."

I was fascinated by the idea, but to practice it with my daughters, according to how I had heard it explained at the conference, I realized I would have to let go of my agenda of wise words and old lessons. I would have to trust them to tell me what truly mattered. I would have to let them find their own voices and try to understand what their hearts were truly feeling.

The subsequent effect on our relationship was slow and subtle. The first changes were mostly on my side. I started to enjoy "heart listening," which was focused, peaceful, and relaxing. I began to understand my daughters on a much deeper level. There was less need to go places and do things or buy stuff. They even seemed to enjoy just doing nothing, as long as we were together. I kept urging them to invite friends along, but they seemed to prefer special time just for us.

During one particular summer week, we created a wonderful bedtime ritual. A half-hour before sunset, the girls would carry our big pink foam pads out to the deck and position them for a perfect view of the sunset colors, the emerging stars, and the rising moon. I would follow with bedding and pillows. Next came the careful positioning of Ali's incense candles and Emmy's juice. Finally, we would decide which book or stories to read and do a battery check for our flashlight/reading lamp.

We were awed by the beauty around us, and after we lit the candles, we would start to talk:

"Look at how fluffy and pink the clouds are, and there's one that looks like Mickey Mouse."

"Look, the first star . . . and there's another one."

"The first person who sees a falling star gets to make a special wish."

"Daddy, how do the crickets make that noise?"

"Daddy, there's a deer . . . and there's a fawn!"

Gradually there was a shift to more personal topics:

"Daddy, when are you going to publish those children's stories? Can I help you write them?"

"I don't think I like Melissa as much as I used to. It's not the same when she comes over anymore."

I would lie there as still as I could and practice "heart listening," although I still had to bite my tongue to curtail all the interruptions, comments, and advice that kept popping into my head. I felt a new closeness and a deeper understanding—a heart connection. I wanted the evenings to last forever.

Finally, one of the girls would say, "Let's read," and we would take turns passing the book and the flashlight around. An hour or so later I'd be startled back awake with the girls' laughter because old Dad had fallen asleep in mid-word, dropping the book and flashlight. Then some soft "I love you's" and "Look! the moon is up," a squeeze on my arm, and I would wake up to the sounds of songbirds and the first soft morning colors.

I was working half-days that week and wouldn't see the girls until afternoon. I knew they would wake up a couple of hours after I had left the house, so I would leave a new "love" message for them on the bathroom counter every morning. Though they never said a word about the notes all week long, I always smiled inside at about nine when I knew they would discover what I had written.

On the day that they had to return to their mother's house, I included a question in my messages: "Of all the things we have done together this week, what have you enjoyed the most?" Their replies were keepers. Here's part of Ali's:

> Daddy, I can't tell you how much I have enjoyed
> this week. Most of all, I enjoyed finding your love
> notes every morning, how we share and talk, and
> our time on the deck. I love you more every day, and
> I can hardly wait to get back here. Ali.

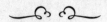

My girls still don't have friends here, no basketball team, no dance class. But our relationship is better than ever. Growing up is never easy to do. Adolescence brings its own special set of issues. How I relish the fact that my daughters are usually willing to talk them out with me, rather than hide their confusion or fear a scolding.

I am convinced I could not do anything more powerful than "heart listen" to my daughters. Like all of us, kids yearn to have someone really listen to them, to be understood, to be honored for their thoughts and feelings. What has amazed me the most is how much children will share when they have a safe place to be heard and can be honest with their feelings. And if listening is a gift I can give my daughters, the greatest reward I receive in return is the lifetime bond I see growing stronger every day.

Bottle Talk
Marilou and Earl Pearce
Fayetteville, North Carolina

When our twin girls, Rebecca and Rachel, were about three years old, we decided it was time they gave up their bottles, which they seemed to love more than anything in this world. We thought of many ways to get rid of the bottles but failed time and time again. It was getting close to Christmas when we hatched the perfect plan.

We sat the girls down on Christmas Eve and told them that Santa was coming with big-girl toys and that it would be a great idea if we could help him with his gift-giving. Little babies need bottles, we said, so we put a paper bag by the fireplace, and the girls placed all their bottles in the bag so Santa could take them to a little baby for Christmas.

The girls went to bed that night as excited about the new toys they were going to get as they were about helping Santa with a baby's present. But about thirty minutes later they came to us crying. When we asked them what was the matter, their answer surprised us. "We don't want Santa to bring us any toys this year," they wailed. "We want to keep our bottles. Tell Santa to take our presents somewhere else but leave our bottles here!"

We were speechless but realized that they were not ready to give up their precious bottles. We had tried to manipulate them and had ignored their true feelings. Their compromise was to each take one bottle to keep and Santa could have the rest. They went to bed happy.

Several weeks later they came to us and said it was time to let the trashman have the two remaining bottles. They threw them away themselves without any urging from us. How much easier it is when you listen to how your children really feel.

Training Wheels, Training Ears
Noreen Broering
Fife Lake, Michigan

It was one of those beautiful early spring days, and after I had an especially stressful afternoon at work, I eagerly anticipated exchanging my high heels for running shoes and enjoying the great outdoors. I picked up my daughter, Ashley, at day care, drove home, and got ready to run. I told Ashley she could ride her bike, and I would run alongside her. She looked at me and firmly announced, "No way am I riding that bike with those training wheels on it. I'm five years old now."

Not listening, I took off running, expecting her to follow. Of course, she dug her heels in and just stood there next to her bike with the detested training wheels. As the minutes passed and she still refused to ride, I became angrier and angrier. The beautiful afternoon suddenly turned very ugly, and we returned home.

Finally, after I had calmed down, my daughter approached me and asked, "Has all that anger gone out of you now, Mommy?"

"Yes," I replied. We sat down to talk about the situation, and I finally listened to my daughter. She said she felt that she was much too old for training wheels. After all, her best friend, Katie, could ride her bike without them. We proceeded to plan our strategy for Ashley to learn how to ride her bike without the training wheels. And you can be sure I listened then.

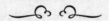

I sn't it remarkable how life works when we just listen? And how high the cost is when we don't?

A Walk Around the Playground
Vern M.
Seattle, Washington

Poor Samuel. That's how we always thought of him. Never Sam. No, he couldn't be just plain Sam. Always "Samuel" in class and "poor Samuel" in our hearts and minds. Not that he was poor as in welfare poor. The son of a single mother, yes, but one who was working hard to provide what he needed. Still, it was only the second half of fourth grade, and he was already beyond her control.

Sullen Samuel. Sarcastic Samuel. Screaming Samuel. Skipping school Samuel. This was a kid who was far along the road to failure. And if we couldn't help him through fourth grade, God help him when he was out on the streets.

After a choking incident on the playground, expulsion seemed pretty likely. But, we reasoned, that would have put him out on those bleak streets even sooner—or, if he was lucky, only in juvenile hall.

Finally, he was diagnosed with Attention Deficit Disorder, and help through medication was on its way, we prayed. But not for Samuel. His mom still dragged him to school every morning, kicking and screaming the whole way. He refused to take his medicine and sat scowling all day, arms crossed, refusing to cooperate. The other kids didn't like him, we didn't like him, and he clearly didn't like himself much, either.

Then one day he was in the principal's office for the umpteenth time and seemed more out of control than ever. He was screaming and resisting so defiantly that Mr. Martin had to struggle to keep him under control with a powerful bear hug that even wiry Samuel couldn't escape, although he certainly tried.

"You jerk principal," he screamed. "You asshole. This is abuse. I'm going to report you. I want to call the cops. You can't do this to me. Call the cops."

"Yes, please do call the police," Mr. Martin calmly said to his secretary.

As poor Samuel's feeling-pretty-ineffective counselor, I had to sit in on the conversation when the police officer arrived.

"What's bothering you, son?" he asked.

"He was beating me up," Samuel said, his snarl not endearing him to anyone.

"I was holding him, yes," Mr. Martin agreed.

"No, he was abusing me. I know abuse. He was hurting me."

"What do you want me to do?" the officer asked the squirming boy.

"Arrest him. He abuses kids. He's mean." Samuel was beginning to get a little quieter.

"What else do you want?"

"Nothing." Defiant Samuel was speaking.

"You can ask for anything. Let's see what we can work out," the officer continued.

"Naw. No one cares anyway. Grown-ups just tell you stuff." Sullen Samuel was still there.

"So, what do you really want? Give us a list of everything you want."

What a simple question—and one that no one had ever asked Samuel sincerely, let alone listen to his answers. He decided to test their challenge.

A chance to eat lunch with his mom once a week on her day off? Easy to arrange.

Shoot hoops one-on-one with the PE teacher? Of course.

And, most of all, talk to a man every week? "Which man?" we asked.

Poor Samuel—no, by now it was pleading, almost silent Samuel who pointed shyly at the principal.

For the next two years their ten-minute walks around the playground every Friday were a sacred ritual. Mr. Martin rarely talked, but he listened so hard that he often joked his ears hurt.

We all applauded just plain Samuel when he headed off to middle school.

For five years now we've all spent a whole lot more time listening. Ten-minute walks are common not only for the principal but also for the teachers and counselors. I kept wishing there were more of us because there are so many needy kids. But help has arrived today.

This morning I'm looking forward to my first meeting with a group of student mentors from the high school. It has been a flourishing program in a neighboring district, which pairs successful, motivated upperclassmen with troubled elementary and middle school students. It helps out where there are not enough adults around to listen to, to play with, to care for, and to encourage these kids, because the mean streets are still out there, waiting to claim them as casualties unless someone can shoot a few hoops or just "walk around the playground" with them.

The fresh-faced, eager high schoolers file in behind their advisor, pin on their name tags, and find a seat at the big table. I look up from the notes I've been reviewing and start to greet them. "Good morning, Mariah. Did I pronounce that right? Good morning, Kevin . . . Ryan . . . Hannah . . . Jenelle. Good morning, uh . . ." My eyes shift to the other side of the table, seeking the next name tag. "Good morning, Samuel."

CHAPTER EIGHT
The Gift of Communication

~&ↄ~

Speaking the Truth of Love
Maureen Ritter
Medina, New York

This wasn't supposed to happen to us. It was supposed to be one of the happiest days of our lives. We had all waited so long and with such anticipation. I took good care of myself during this pregnancy, and I prayed to God for another healthy, perfect baby. Still, I worried because I was over forty years old and knew the statistics and that certain risks might be involved. I even said a special nightly prayer so that this baby wouldn't have Down's syndrome—anything but that! But through all my pre-natal exams and sonograms, my OB-GYN assured us that our son was developing just fine and gave us no cause for concern or uncertainty. My husband, Bob, was thrilled. We had tried for more than a year to conceive, and I knew how his heart ached for a child of our own. At thirty-six this was his first child, and his dream was finally coming true.

I had two boys by my previous marriage. My older son, Aaron, was sixteen and was unselfishly accepting and excited about my having a baby. In fact, he thought it was pretty cool. My younger son, Ryan, was especially excited. He had been "my baby" for twelve years now, and finally he was going to be a big brother like Aaron. In fact, that was how Ryan made our announcement to family and friends; "I'm going to be a big brother!" not the more traditional, "Mom's going to have a baby."

Ryan has many wonderful attributes, but I especially enjoy his unique and witty sense of humor, his sensitive nature (needing my comforting arms when his feelings get hurt), his quick willingness to forgive, his creative and vivid imagination that is reflected in his artwork and play, his haunting green eyes, lavish eyelashes, and wavy blond hair, his innocent impish pranks (of which I am usually the victim), and also his loving nature that makes him always generous with his affection.

During my pregnancy, I never tired of Ryan's endless questions about the baby. We frequently enjoyed looking at his and Aaron's baby photos while I told him amusing and memorable stories of when they were little. I've always been very sentimental and saved all my boys' baby clothes, toys, and infant paraphernalia, including Ryan's "ba-bas." I treasured these hours of sharing reminiscences with Ryan.

Since most of our conversations had become focused on the baby, I often wondered if and when Ryan might begin displaying signs of jealousy. Would his title of big brother lose its excitement within weeks? How will he react when the baby demands all my time and energy? Will we ever be this close again? Will he love his new brother? Will he understand I won't love him any less? But I felt reassured as Ryan often talked about all the things he and his little brother were going to do together, the places they would go, the fun they would have, and everything he would teach him.

Ryan also spent many hours in our attic carefully sorting his accumulation of Matchbox vehicles, G.I. Joes, Masters of the Universe, Teenage Mutant Ninja Turtles, and Tonka trucks. Originally, he had planned to sell everything at a yard sale and keep all the profits. But now he had generously decided that he wanted his baby brother to inherit his collections.

On January 4, 1993, Dane Robert was born. In the delivery room no one said, "Congratulations" or "He's beautiful" or made any other remarks. The doctor hastily went about his postdelivery routine while the nurses quietly attended to our new son. In retrospect, I thought the room was unusually quiet but didn't know why. Dane had ten beautiful little fingers and toes, a full head of blond hair, and looked like a typical newborn to me. So precious. Bob and I were ecstatic.

My doctor interrupted that joyous moment by stating that our pediatrician was unable to examine Dane, but there was one available on staff. We agreed to let him see Dane. Within ten minutes a pediatrician, a total stranger with a heavy foreign accent, entered, introduced himself, and stated matter-of-factly, "Your baby has Down's syndrome, okay?" Then he turned and left.

Okay? No, it was not okay. I was devastated! My first thoughts were: Mongoloid idiot. That's what people will call him. God has betrayed me! What about all those months of prayers for a healthy, normal baby? Oh, Bob, how could I give you a son like this? It isn't fair. It can't be true. This is a nightmare. How could I be such a failure? I've given us a lifetime of inconceivable hardship, misery, heartbreak, anguish, frustration, and "those looks" from people for the rest of our lives. What was I trying to prove having a baby at my age? Bob and I held each other tightly as our tears flowed relentlessly.

Eventually, I was put in a private room to bear my sorrow alone. As my heavy heart was breaking for a future that would never be, I thought of Aaron and Ryan. How will they feel? How will they react? Could they ever forgive me? Would they want to? Will all of Ryan's dreams be shattered, too?

As I wallowed inconsolably in self-pity and pity for a baby who had no room in my perfect little world, Aaron and Ryan entered. I cried and begged their forgiveness for giving them an inferior burden, but Ryan glared at me with his beautiful green eyes, grasped my shoulders firmly, and announced lovingly but decisively, "Mom, what is the problem? We've waited a long time for Dane. I love him, and we're going to keep him!"

Ryan displayed no sorrow, no pity, no shame, no anger, no

sense of betrayal by God. He spoke only of unconditional love and acceptance. And at that moment I realized the day was not a nightmare or a punishment or a failure.

How could I have felt all those spiteful thoughts about little Dane? Because of Ryan I was able to arrive at acceptance, and my self-pity vanished. I realized that I should rejoice in this new and "special" life we had waited a long time for, whom we loved and were going to keep.

Since Dane's birth three years ago, Ryan has spent countless hours each week with his little brother. He has sacrificed being with his friends, playing most school sports, and having his own personal time to be with and take care of Dane. Ryan doesn't consider this a burden. In fact, many professionals agree that he has done more for Dane's physical development than any therapist through their constant interaction and physical play involving athletics and rough-and-tumble activities. Dane adores Ryan, and they share a unique and special bond of brotherly love.

How could Ryan have known how much joy Dane would bring into all our lives? I've learned a lesson about life, about Ryan, and about myself. Life is unjust at times. Events happen to us that seem unfair or undeserved. The way we react, accept, and deal with life makes us who we are. It can bring out the best or the worst in us.

When Dane was born, the shocking diagnosis we were totally unprepared for brought out the worst in me. It brought out the best in Ryan. He could have said anything to me that day or said nothing. What he did say made all the difference to me. This unassuming, loving, sincere child chose to remind me that love has no limits or boundaries depending on one's handicap. How wise, how mature, how true!

Only those families who have children with special needs can fully understand and appreciate the love and joy they bring to a family. To many, Dane's accomplishments may seem minor or insignificant. To us, each achievement is cause for celebration.

We are very fortunate to have Dane, his sweet disposition, his smiles and laughter, and his constant affection. As we teach Dane, he teaches us. He, like Ryan, has taught us what is truly important in life.

What does it mean to speak the truth of love, to speak authentically instead of role-playing or jockeying for position? Children like Ryan demonstrate that when true, loving communication happens, our lives change.

I've found that when I can communicate openly and fully, barriers come down. How alive can we be if we have to shut down the most meaningful parts of ourselves? People who make a difference in the world speak from the heart.

Talk to Me, Grandpa
Janet E. Smith
Greeley, Colorado

For several weeks after my father's stroke, we kept his only grandchild, my niece Desiree, from seeing him. She was only three. It was difficult, however, because Desiree and her grandfather had a very special relationship. She longed to see him; she missed laughing and dancing with him, and talking the way that only grandpas and granddaughters can.

Dad underwent weeks of intensive rehabilitation. Progress was slow as he relearned simple daily living skills. He was most anxious to regain his speech. Therapists worked with him daily, and after several weeks he was able to utter his first word, "Hi!" We were delighted at this hopeful sign and decided that Desiree could now see her Grandpa. Her mother had prepared her for the meeting. "Grandpa can't walk," she explained. "He has to use a wheelchair." Far more difficult, however, was explaining that Grandpa could no longer talk.

The day came. We wheeled Dad outside so we could gather in a comfortable spot. Desiree approached him like someone trying to catch a butterfly approaches the bush where it has lighted. With cautious excitement she walked up to Grandpa and hugged him as gently as she could, working around the wheelchair's appendages. Dad labored to lean toward Desiree and stuttered out his only word, "Hi!" We all exhaled in relief to see things going well.

Her natural curiosity guided Desiree as she studied her grandpa and us. We all tried to act "normal" for both their sakes, though we were painfully aware that life would never be "normal" again. Then it happened: a sweet, innocent question that had to be asked. Desiree tiptoed up to her grandpa and softly pleaded, "Won't you talk with me, Grandpa?" She only wanted what they had once shared. We all only wanted what we once had. But only Desiree had the courage to ask the question that was in all our hearts. We quickly changed the subject, afraid to upset Grandpa and not knowing how to explain the situation any further to Desiree.

After months of rehabilitation, Dad was finally able to come home. Though he had only a little movement in his right side, he had regained some speech. He searched for words, but once again he and his now five-year-old granddaughter could carry on special conversations.

Looking back, Desiree's boldness taught us how important it is to search honestly for answers to life's tragedies. Why should we not ask those burning questions? Instead of burying our fears in "appropriate behavior," why not speak of the pain from which such questions arise? If adults handled hardship with childlike vulnerability, we would work through our grief far more quickly. May the courageous innocence of children be our teacher.

A Simple Gift of Hello
Maryl Kacir
Royal Oak, Michigan

When my eighteen-month-old daughter, Jorah, says hello, miracles happen. Time passes joyfully in long lines at the post office. Busy executives relax their shoulders and take a moment to smile. When her voice floats across a restaurant to a friend, everyone in the room is washed in a wave of lightness.

One morning I realized I had ordered the wrong bank checks. But I didn't want to pay for my mistake, so I practiced my excuses and hoped the same bank clerk wouldn't be there when I returned the checks.

At the bank I pushed Jorah in her stroller to the customer service area, and there sat the same bank clerk. I pretended not to see her, but my daughter's voice reached across the room and landed right on her desk. "Hello," Jorah said, as if the clerk were the most important person in the room.

The bank clerk smiled. "I remember you," she said and waved us over to her desk. I realized then that she was a human being after all. I could admit I made a mistake, and everything would be okay. The bank exchanged the checks for new ones without charge. And I was grateful for a chance to learn a lesson in humility without too much pain—all because of the power of Jorah's hello. The meaning of the word has changed forever for me.

I used to use the word as a tool to get what I wanted or as a weapon for self-defense. Saying hello on a rough city street meant "Please pass me by without hurting me." In my own neighborhood, if I ever said hello, it meant "I know my space; I belong." At stores it meant "I'm here. Pay attention to my needs." On the phone it was "What do you want?"

Now I hear my daughter say, "Hello," and I see what it really means. To the man with the briefcase hurrying by, it says, "A ray of sunshine beams between you and me. All things in it are sparkling and special." To the grocer with bruised bananas it says, "I know your secret desire is to smile at everyone, so start with me." To the woman slumped on the bus stop bench it says, "Your deepest troubles will fall from your hands if you open them to wave at me."

All these people are stopped by one word: hello.

When I walk down the street now, I feel as if I've been given the freedom to love a stranger and the power to change someone's life. Whenever I greet people, I can see humanity in their faces and can sense a new joy-filled attitude in my own life. Jorah taught me the *real* meaning of hello.

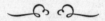

C ommunication is very much a two-way street—not only do our children teach us, but we teach them.

Stupid Cast!
Carole Persons
Steamboat Springs, Colorado

When our granddaughter, Nicholle, was three, she fell and broke her arm. She handled the pain, the emergency room, the X rays —all the unpleasantness associated with a broken bone. The cast, however, was a source of extreme humiliation and embarrassment to her. She did not want anyone to notice it, would not allow anyone to sign it, and actually cried and ran to hide when someone mentioned it. "Everybody will say I'm stupid," she kept saying, sobbing uncontrollably every time someone noticed the cast.

We were stunned. How could she believe that anyone would say such a thing? Finally, her mother's sister figured it out. A few months before her accident, Nicholle's dad had broken a bone in his hand when he lost his temper and hit his horse! Of course, people gave him a bad time about it, kidding him and saying what a dumb thing to do! Apparently, Nicholle had associated being dumb or stupid with a cast, and she had filed it away in her young and impressionable mind.

It was a painful lesson, but we learned that it is not just the words we say directly to a child that matter. The way adults treat one another also shapes the way children see themselves!

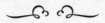

The gift of communication comes quite naturally to children. They are eager to tell us everything. It is their way of exploring and expressing their feelings. We cannot take that gift for granted. If it is not welcomed and appreciated, it will simply be withdrawn, and we will miss out on the things that are important in their lives.

The Jeffrey Story
Gary and Ann McAfee
Cicero, New York

Truly the most delightful part of our lives has been watching our son Jeffrey, grow. Our only regret is that over these past seven years we have often found ourselves missing out on many of his achievements because of work demands. But one night, purely by accident, we came up with a way in which Jeffrey could proudly share with us his accomplishments each and every day.

Jeffrey was nearly two years old at the time. Each night we read him a couple of bedtime stories. On this particular night, however, after we had finished the first book, Jeffrey asked if we could make up a story to tell him. As we tucked him into bed, we began, "Once upon a time, there was a little boy named Jeffrey . . ." and this was the beginning of *The Jeffrey Story*.

Ann helped Jeff recall his day's activities for me. The excitement in his eyes was precious as he told me his story. Now, six years later, *The Jeffrey Story* has become a bedtime tradition, allowing our son the opportunity to help us experience all the tremendous tales of a little boy's life. Ann and I now know that despite how our day goes and no matter what activities we might be involved in, we will always be able to end the day in our son's world—right where we belong.

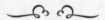

I shudder to think of how many times I have treated my kids as if they were invisible instead of the human beings they are. Of how many times they have protested and cried because what I was really communicating was: "Kids, you do not matter. Your thoughts are not important. Your feelings are not my concern. Ask your opinion? Give me a break. You're just a kid."

An incident at a friend's house one afternoon taught me the importance of the gift of two-way communication.

The blinking light on the answering machine seemed to pulse with special urgency one sunny afternoon as my friend, his two boys, Eric and Alex, and I trooped into their condo after an exciting morning of soccer. Seven-year-old Eric hurried to play the message, an eager smile on his face. But smiles quickly turned sour on both his and his brother's faces as their mother's voice boomed through the speaker.

"Eric, Alex, don't plan anything more with your father this weekend. I can't come to get you, but I've arranged for someone else to pick you up. He'll be coming two hours earlier than we had originally planned."

The boys called her back. They pleaded: "We don't want

to go home early. We have a cool video to watch, and Dad has a new game on his computer we get to try." It was no use. "She says she can't change her plans now just for us," Alex told his father after he hung up the phone.

Another call a few minutes later. The boys were crying by now. "But, Mom, we don't know who this guy is. We're scared to ride with him. Will he make us listen to icky music? What if he's boring? That's a long ride back to your town."

But again their mother refused to listen. "She says this is the way it has to be," Eric sobbed. "Daddy, I don't want to go. I don't care if I do have to go to school tomorrow. I want to stay here with you."

My friend, who had tried so valiantly to stay out of the fray and let the boys work things out with their mother, sat down to listen. "What do you want your mom to do?" he said.

"Just ask us," they both replied. "Make her stop ordering us to do everything." My friend was heading for the phone as I ran out to pick up some ice-cream treats at the corner convenience store. The tension was getting too much for me.

The boys were in a very different mood when I got back, and I knew it wasn't the ice-cream bars that had them smiling. "What happened?" I asked.

My friend explained: "She asked the boys which they would prefer. She could come and get them, or they could ride with this friend who was a very safe driver and she would have time to make their favorite dinner and get a copy of that video they wanted to watch. And she was open to any other suggestions they might have."

"Yeah," Eric chimed in. "She actually asked us."

—◦ ◦—

Kaitlyn wrote the following poem after hearing a friend of her mother's recalling the pain he felt as a child when he was referred to only as a number.

Locket
Kaitlyn Talmage-Bowers, age 11
Denver, Colorado

Listening, straining your ears just to hear Mother's voice.
In with another—brother or sister. Number three, you think.
Is that a way to call your children, by numbers instead of
      names?
You wait, you listen, silence, followed again by everlasting
      silence.
Your life is locked in a box and Mother holds the key.
You call out a pleading cry. "Not now!" booms Mother's voice.
Not much, but at least it is more than silence.
The other child feels for you the pain in one moment.
She wants to run and comfort you.
Then she thinks, "Why? I'm here now in precious mother's time,
      my time."
Minutes pass.
The soft pat of Mother's shoes, the sweet smell of her perfume
      passes you
and all the others' doors. They all hold their breath.
She picks a door and enters.
All let out their breath and again sit in silence.
Listening, waiting, hoping. Listening, waiting, hoping.

Listening, waiting, hoping.
Again and again. *

The Hug
As told to Bill Skewes by his father, Mort B. Skewes
Luverne, Minnesota

I was born in 1908 into a hardworking and undemonstrative English/German farm family. My father never called me by name, just "kid." I plowed my share of fields behind a team of mules, but I was determined not to be a farmer. I became a lawyer, but unfortunately, setting up a law practice during the Depression required working long hours—most nights until midnight and weekends as well.

During his formative years, Bill spent a lot of time with my dad and my dad's brother. In many ways they were my son's father substitutes. Dad died when Bill was twenty-one, and he sobbed uncontrollably during the funeral. I wondered whether he would feel the same when I died. I realized that I could not recall ever giving my son a hug or even pitching him a ball.

My daughter and son grew up and went off to college before I ever had much time with them. Now Mary, our daughter, lives in North Carolina, and Bill, our son, is in Colorado. My wife, Mildred, and I are truly alone, and the emptiness is excruciating. I ache that I never took the time to know my children.

Both of them now have families of their own. We haven't seen them very often, and when we did, it was very businesslike. We shook hands when we met and when we parted. Our talk was mostly politics.

Whenever I was around Bill, I noticed that he hugged his children a lot. Obviously he didn't learn that from our family.

---

* (Reprinted with permission from *Serendipity*, the literary magazine for The Logan School for Creative Learning, Denver, Colorado.)

But I was left with a sense of loss, of an insurmountable distance from my own children.

In 1988, as Mildred and I got ready to leave after a pleasant visit with my son and his delightful family, I extended my hand to Bill as usual. He moved his hand toward mine, then stopped. He hesitated, took a step closer, reached out his arm, and gave me a hug! Tears blinded me. Here I was eighty years old and was only now sharing this family intimacy. It felt wonderful!

Now, I never miss a hug. I only wish it hadn't taken me so long to understand what I had missed all those years. Had I known, well, maybe I could have shared love with my father. I wish I had had the chance.

The gift of communication comes in many forms—a hug, a smile, a kiss. But the expression in words of their love and gratitude, whatever the language, is surely one of the most precious gifts that children give their parents.

Gracias
Dawn Shepherd, Public Housing Authority Director
Denver, Colorado

Areli Mancera rose to accept her scholarship from San Francisco's mayor, Willie Brown, Jr., as hundreds of well-wishers applauded her success so far in life. The fourth of seven children born to farmworkers, she was an honor student with a 4.3 grade point average on a 4.0 scale, ranking her fourth in a class of two hundred. She was president of the Organization for Raza, Achievement, Leadership and Education; vice president of the American Field Service; a member of the Student Congress and

Girls' State, and on the honor roll—and she still managed to work ten to twenty hours a week to help her family.

I was glad that cauliflower wasn't on the menu for today's luncheon, because Areli had also spent many hot, miserable, backbreaking hours in the fields with her family tying cauliflower.

Each year the Public Housing Authority's Directors Association awarded a scholarship to a deserving student who lived in public housing. This was Areli's year to receive the $3,000 Bollinger award.

I listened raptly to her touching thank-you speech:

My name is Areli Mancera. I am the daughter of Jose and Susana Mancera. I live in the town of Chualar, California, located in the Salinas Valley, known to many as the world's salad bowl. I graduated from Gonzales High School and plan to attend the University of California, Santa Cruz.

At a very young age my father and mother impressed upon my brothers, sister, and me to pursue an education. They have always said, "Work with your head, not your back" such as they—who for over twenty-five years have had to endure the strenuous physical conditions of laboring in agriculture. With an education, my parents believe, we children can avoid such hardships. This is why my siblings and I try to excel in our education, thereby repaying my parents' efforts and making them feel very proud.

Areli went on to express her appreciation for the scholarship because her parents' income would never have allowed higher education. There were not many dry eyes in the room as she paid tribute to all those who had helped her. Here was a young woman dedicating her life to becoming a teacher and role model for young people. We began to applaud until we realized she had not quite finished her talk.

She turned to face her parents, love and gratitude radiating from her face:

Mama, Papa, primeramente quiciera darles las gracias por traerme aquí a San Francisco. Con este gesto, me demuestran lo importante que somos sus hijos y nuestra educación.

I suddenly remembered that her parents did not speak English. They had probably understood only a fraction of the tribute she had given them in her speech.

Les quiero dar las gracias por todo el apoyo que han brindado a mí y a mis hermanos. También les quiero dar a saber que les agradesco por los morales, principios, y valores que nos han inculcado. . . . Mother, Father, thank you for all the support you have given me since the day I entered this world. All the morals and values you have taught me have made me become a person of good, and I thank you from the bottom of my heart. I hope with God's guidance, and also your own, I will continue on the right path and make everyone proud, including myself.

CHAPTER NINE

The Gift of Trust

~ ❧ ~

A Hand in the Cookie Jar
Laurie Larabell
Walled Lake, Michigan

I reddened as I rounded the corner of our kitchen to find my six-year-old daughter perched on a chair next to the refrigerator, grasping a container of candy. She jumped when I asked, "Danielle, what are you doing?"

"Nothing, Mama," she answered. "Guilty" was written all over her face.

Misjudging her expression, I assumed she was sneaking candy from her treat bowl. "Danielle, tell me the truth. Did you eat any candy?" I demanded.

"No," she answered in a soft voice, posture stilted, staring straight ahead.

"Danielle, I mean it. What are you doing?"

"Nothing, really, Mama," she said, eyes now downcast, slowly turning her head as if this confrontation suddenly required that she memorize the dimensions of the kitchen floor.

"You know you must ask me before taking candy," I went on. Sensing she was holding something back, I pressed the issue, interrogating her as she got off the chair. Following her into the dining room, I continued to fire questions at her until she broke down with a confession.

I then discovered that surprise, not guilt, was the reason for her startled expression—the look one has when caught wrapping a present or planning a surprise party when the intended walks into the room. I discovered I had caught Danielle in the act of making an elaborate Christmas present for me.

I stared into her sad eyes as she started to explain. That morning, rising two hours before me, she had diligently begun to cut paper into confetti with her scissors. She was planning to present me with a large bag on Christmas Eve, brimming with paper fluff from which I would select gifts chosen from her own collection of treasures, including delicacies from her treat bowl.

Crouching behind the dining room door, Danielle lifted the evidence into view. It was a red shopping bag with a recycled pink satin ribbon tied on the handles. When she invited me to reach into the bag, my hand touched some of her favorite pieces of jewelry and various other collectibles, ranging from erasers to postcards. The gift was complete except for three pieces of chocolate from her treat bowl that she still clutched in her fist.

I felt horrible. Included in the cache was a card she had written for me that said, "Dear Mommy, Have a happy Christmas and happy present, Love, Danielle M." Her surreptitious plan was foiled, but not in vain. The honesty and pure-hearted generosity of her gift worked like a vaccine, filling my veins with a dose of humility, love, sharing, and forgiveness. There was a squeezing vise in my chest as I began, "Danielle, I'm so sorry . . ."

Though this may seem like a small incident (let's face it, we all have bad days), for me it was a revelation. Here was a child behaving first with creativity and love, then with maturity and self-confidence. Danielle never became angry or reproachful; her only concern was my hurt feelings and her inability to surprise me on Christmas Eve.

I am proud to say that my daughter conveyed an unmistakable message that day: I have a great kid, and she deserves my trust. Of course my reaction was logical, but my mistake taught me a big lesson about trust. And thanks to Danielle, I'm realigned, rejuvenated—and I can't wait to catch someone else's hand in the cookie jar.

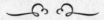

I t's amazing to me how children tend to trust first while adults tend to doubt and blame first. My colleague, Pandora, related a perfect example from her teen years.

"When I was thirteen," she told me, "my friend and I went to a movie by ourselves for the first time. Like many multiplex theaters, the exit emptied into an alley, and by chance, my friend's dad met us coming around the back of the building toward the parking lot. He went ballistic. 'I knew I couldn't trust you,' he yelled. 'What were you doing back there?'

"He was so hung up on his doubting and judging that he refused to listen to an explanation," Pandora continued. "I could see how my friend's relationship with her parents changed from that point on. She knew they thought she wasn't good or trustworthy, so that's exactly the script she followed."

What a difference it would make if we learned to trust first, to judge on intent rather than appearances.

I recently attended a meeting with three executives from a large telecommunications conglomerate.

"I want to make sure we launch the '97 products with a more sophisticated campaign. . . ."

"I just heard from our Salt Lake City branch that they can't keep up with the demand. . . ."

"I really need to beef up my department. Forget marketing. We have got to funnel every extra dollar into the work they're doing. Their equipment is a joke. . . ."

My head swiveled from one speaker to another. They all had their own business and personal agendas, but it was easy to see that they needed one another's input and support to accomplish their common overall objective. Talk filled the room for an hour and a half, but real listening only happened for about a minute and a half. Demand followed demand, and maybe every third or fourth statement vaguely related to something that had been said before—but usually only to dismiss it as irrelevant or unworthy.

One person mistrusted everybody else's intention and was afraid his needs wouldn't be considered. The next felt as if the other team members were jockeying for their own status or selfish needs. Another didn't trust himself to speak his own mind and therefore looked for everyone else's weakness so he could have the advantage.

It was a meeting that did more harm than good. It destroyed trust and self-esteem, and nothing was accomplished. These high-powered executives set out to accomplish a basic marketing plan, and instead they got pain and disrespect, and ended up several steps behind where they were when they entered the room.

As I was sitting there watching this disturbing and destructive meeting, I couldn't help but wonder what would have happened if every person there had made a commitment to actually listen to each other in an atmosphere of trust and understanding.

How much better our lives would be if we as adults could regain the trust that children display so naturally.

Flight of the Red Balloon
Anne Brady Baxter
Hattiesburg, Mississippi

Last month my only uncle died. I will be forever grateful that I, along with my five-year-old son, James, had the opportunity to visit him just days before his death. During the days that followed, James could sense my sadness. I believe that because children's minds are not clouded with all the mundane and often trivial affairs of the world, they are capable of much keener perception into the hearts and souls of others. I suppose it's some form of intuition that we adults have selectively erased from our nervous system.

When we arrived home late one afternoon about a week later, James was the proud owner of a bright red helium-filled balloon, probably given to him by a bank, a mall, or a pizzeria. As we walked up the steps to the front door, he stopped and said in a soft voice, "I want to send this balloon up to Uncle Bill."

I froze on the steps, struck by the truth of such a simple remark. In the mind of the five-year-old, Uncle Bill was not really dead; rather, he was alive and well in some other place and would be delightfully appreciative of a bright red balloon. He lived on in an innocent, unclouded mind which had no conception that the beauty and wonder of life can ever be terminated.

James let go of the string on the red balloon, and as fate—or, rather, the shift of the winds—would have it, the red balloon became lodged in the branches of a tree. Horror swept across James's eyes. The significance of the failed mission of the red balloon could not be expressed in a five-year-old's vocabulary.

The next morning James bounded downstairs and rushed toward the front door with wide eyes, asking, "Is it still there?"

As we opened the door, all we saw were green leaves. The bright red balloon was nowhere in sight. James was ecstatic. "It's gone to Uncle Bill in heaven!" he exclaimed, dancing with joy.

Where the balloon actually came to rest is unknown. It is

not a mystery to James, however; he knows and does not question the balloon's destination. I wish we could all know without question.

I'm often dismayed by the many risk factors that children face: broken families, poverty, lack of education, an uncaring community, single-parent families. Study after study has found that kids who have one or two of these factors working against them are at the greatest risk for teenage pregnancy, crime, drugs, violence, and gang activity. Even worse, more and more children are being exposed to these risks.

Even in the midst of all these perils, however, some "pearls" have bolstered my hope. Researchers have identified several "wellness" or protective factors that reduce young people's chances of getting into trouble. Without question the most important of these is having a bond with an adult who loves them unconditionally, listens deeply, and honors their feelings. And nothing creates a deeper bond between a child and an adult than trust.

Sorry, No Santa
Cindy Bartlett
Waverly, Nebraska

The first Christmas season after my husband and I had separated was rough. I didn't take my almost-six-year-old daughter, Heidi, to visit Santa Claus and didn't even talk about what she and her brother Nick wanted. Money was too tight. Instead, we talked about not asking Santa for quite so many gifts that year and other ways we could enjoy their birthdays and Christmas (which all occur between December 17 and January 17). "But, Mom," Heidi said, "I don't believe in Santa. I believe in you!"

Long Years' Journey into Life
Susan Baile
Boulder, Colorado

My older son, Chris, was born without complications, but his brother, Trevor, was severely asphyxiated during his birth. Shortly afterward he developed seizures, and three times he stopped breathing. After his third resuscitation, he was placed on a ventilator and prepared for transport to a neonatal critical care unit in Denver. I stood by helplessly, watching his tiny, seizing body cling to its tenuous hold on life. I had only one thought, one prayer: God, please let my baby live.

In Denver my prayer was answered. The seizures finally stopped, Trevor stabilized, and we knew he would live. Only then did we begin to consider the possible legacy of his birth trauma. Still, I had no idea what it would mean when I made the commitment—first in my heart and then out loud to my son —to do whatever was needed to love and support him. I was elated to be able to take my baby home.

The next five and a half years were marked by celebrations as well as struggles. We celebrated major developmental milestones, Trevor's astonishing ability to sing songs and tell stories verbatim after only brief exposure to them, his unbounded powers of imagination, and, perhaps most of all, a sweetness and radiance that made him an unusually appealing child. On the other hand, Trevor struggled with many everyday tasks that other children his age could do with ease. Finding his lunch table at his preschool, remembering how old he was, catching a large ball from a few feet away, playing simple games—these things would be years away.

Then my daughter, Kenna, was born, two months prematurely. I had the same complication with her that I had with Trevor, but because of my doctor's swift intervention, her health was never compromised as his had been. When Trevor came to see her in the hospital, he sat in a chair across the room from her incubator. He was agitated and irritable. His reaction surprised me, but I chalked it up to ambivalence toward a new sibling. I resolved to spend extra time with him and trusted that his feelings would change as he gained assurance of my continuing love for him.

In the weeks and months following Kenna's birth, though, Trevor became increasingly withdrawn and depressed. Eventually, he became suicidal. For weeks we listened to him insist that he wanted to die, he no longer wanted to be on earth, he was ready to go back to God. On walks he talked about running into the path of oncoming cars. My heart ached to hear this little boy, who had once fought so hard to live, become consumed by this desire to die. I couldn't understand how any little child would want to die, but especially one who had been so deeply loved.

In my utter confusion and unspeakable pain, I blamed myself. Trevor's father and I had divorced, and Kenna had been born very early in my new relationship with Tom. Obviously, I had failed Trevor, and in a big way. Because I blamed myself, I also thought that I could make him well and happy again. So I gave him even more time and attention, convinced that enough love would heal him.

The day that Trevor asked Tom to saw his head off, I knew that his condition required professional help. We found a therapist, and Trevor began working with him. During this time we watched his almost daily deterioration. He had started pacing on tiptoe around and around our kitchen table. When he wasn't pacing, he had begun to stare, in a catatonic-like way, at a wall or at nothing. His preschool teacher informed us that she could no longer care for him; as she put it, "The world has to stop to take care of Trevor."

Then one night while I was putting him to bed, Trevor started screaming. "Save me, save me. I'm dying. My eyes are popping out. I'm dying. Save me. Will I make it to the shore?" His ear-piercing, wild cries continued for more than two hours until at last, exhausted, he collapsed into sleep. The next morning he awoke in a state of acute agitation. His pacing took on a frantic, driven quality. I put a tape on, hoping to soothe him. When the first song ended, he started screaming again.

Soon he screamed uncontrollably anytime a change occurred in his environment: getting in or out of the car, turning the page of a book, needing to go to the bathroom, weather changes—there was no end to the things that could set him off.

By this time our lives had been turned upside down and inside out. Unable to find anyone to care for Trevor (we had hired three baby-sitters who quit, the longest one lasting two days), I stopped working. Since I was the sole financial support for our family at that time, this added one more dimension to our crisis. I spent hours of every day and night holding my screaming, terrified son, rapidly draining myself and ultimately sinking into almost total despair as my family disintegrated. We simply could not go on. I called a crisis center and was referred to a psychiatric hospital for children.

Trevor was admitted to the hospital within an hour with a diagnosis of psychosis and possible autism. I didn't really know what psychosis was, but having a doctor so confidently diagnose Trevor's condition was reassuring. The doctor started Trevor on a very potent medication, promising that it would result in almost immediate relief for him.

During the week of his hospitalization, I read everything I could find on psychosis, childhood depression, and autism. I went to lectures on mental illness and attended a support group for parents of children with severe mental illness. The more I read, the more distressed I became. It simply didn't add up, yet everyone was so sure. I would lie in bed at night wondering if I was in denial and trying to make it all fit together.

A week went by, and Trevor came home. He was no longer

screaming, but as I came to realize, no one would scream after swallowing a dose of the medicine he was taking. He was still totally dysfunctional to the point of needing diapers. And after a few days, he started screaming again. Each day got a little bit worse, until by the end of his third week home, he was screaming as much as he had been when he was first hospitalized. We took him back to the hospital. His medical team admitted being surprised by his response but quickly decided that Trevor's condition required more potent medication. Again he was hospitalized, and again he came home. Also again he deteriorated.

This time when we went back to the hospital, Trevor's doctor told us that he was one of the most seriously disturbed children they had seen in years. Our insurance was running out, and Trevor needed to be someplace where he could heal in his own time and at his own pace. The doctor went on to tell us that Trevor would probably need to be on medication for a long time, perhaps his entire life, and that the chances of his ever living independently were quite low, 10 to 15 percent. He explained to us that Trevor needed to be in the state hospital and urged us to begin the application process immediately.

This was the darkest, most hopeless time of my life. Despite daily pressure from the hospital staff, I was determined not to admit Trevor to the state hospital. I believed that I would lose him forever if I did that. But I also feared losing the rest of my family as I struggled to save Trevor. My relationship with Tom was severely strained; Chris and Kenna were being neglected; we were on the verge of financial disaster; and I was so exhausted that I could barely get up in the morning.

Then a friend gave me the name of a man in California who specialized in birth trauma, and he referred me to a therapist he had trained who lived about an hour away from us. I called Margaret in desperation. She listened while I described Trevor's behavior, then said, "Your son is not psychotic. Your daughter's birth triggered his unconscious memories of his own birth, and he's reexperiencing his birth." Suddenly, everything Trevor had been screaming took on a chilling reality. We had hope.

In our first session, Margaret told me that children tell us what happened to them by their behavior. Trevor, who had been standing by a window, staring vacantly, suddenly walked across the room, put his arms around me, and said, "This is very important." It was the first coherent sentence he had spoken in several months and the beginning of the years of therapy. The therapeutic process required Trevor to go back to the trauma of his birth in order to repattern it.

Margaret would simulate his birth experience by placing him in a fetal position on a mattress, surrounding him with large pillows, then topping the pillows with a blanket. In this dark, womblike environment, Trevor instantaneously reconnected to the agonizing pain, terror, anger, grief, and depression that had characterized his birth. He reenacted elements of his birth that I had forgotten and had never talked about, but they were documented in the medical records, which we received while he was still in therapy.

Trevor knew every time we went to Margaret's that he would literally be scared to death. For the first several months he cried and screamed in the car as we drove to her office. Yet he would begin to work with Margaret almost the moment we walked in the door. It was a gut-wrenching process for both of us, but I think each of us knew in our own way that his future depended on it.

We began to see some changes fairly early on. Trevor was calming down. He started noticing and responding more to his environment. Against medical advice and his doctor's guarantee that he would get worse, we began to wean him off his medications. He kept getting better. The improvements were gradual, but after several months everyone could see that his progress was significant.

Things really began to shift after one particularly poignant therapy session. After many, many failed attempts to urge him to push himself out of his frightening therapeutic "womb," he did it. And as his head and shoulders emerged, he announced in a loud, certain voice, "I claim that I want to live!" When I held

Trevor afterward, I knew that he was coming back. We dissolved into giddy laughter.

We will soon celebrate the first anniversary of the end of Trevor's therapy and the birth of the rest of his life. Not too surprisingly, he is years behind his peers in virtually every arena. Our energy is now directed toward finding ways to support his educational needs. Because of his severe processing problems, we know that his ultimate life choices may be limited.

But Trevor continues to progress, and, emotionally, he is healed. The light in his eyes and the radiance of his being are back. And because we came so close to losing him forever, I find myself profoundly grateful for the smallest things. I am grateful for every morning that he awakens with a smile, and I am grateful for every night that he drifts into sleep with a peaceful heart and mind. And in between I celebrate the ordinariness of our days in a way that would never have occurred to me had Trevor and I not undertaken this extraordinary journey together. We are truly blessed.

As I consider the many lessons of our journey, two seem particularly poignant. The first has to do with pain. It was excruciating to witness the depth of Trevor's agony, and more than anything I wanted to take it away from him. I learned that I could not.

But perhaps more important, I saw that it was Trevor's willingness to fully experience his pain that finally healed him. My ability to trust this lesson was repeatedly challenged by well-meaning professionals who regarded pain-suppressing medications as a necessity, given the severity of his illness. It was hard to stand by and watch his suffering, month after month, knowing that pharmaceutical relief was only a dose away.

I was sustained by Trevor's courage and the almost driven way he went into each therapy session. Eventually, he was able to articulate this lesson for himself; he described a session with Margaret as another opportunity to "send more feelings to the bottom of the sea." He had discovered, at his tender age, the truth that to feel is to heal.

The second lesson I learned is the degree to which our psyches and the unfolding of our lives can be shaped by our earliest experiences, and the incredible cost that can result from ignorance of this fact. I think about the doctors and experts involved in Trevor's care, competent and compassionate people, who could not discern the true source of his condition simply because their belief systems did not include his reality. I have learned that when the behavior of one of my children makes no sense to me—when a response just seems totally inexplicable—it is usually because there is more that I need to understand. It has been humbling to realize how much I don't know, and I realize it is essential to maintain that humility in order to successfully meet the challenges of parenting.

And so our journey continues.

Children who grow up in an atmosphere of trust are not afraid to express their true feelings, to be themselves. Not long ago I was watching some children at a party. It was a typical young people's party—commotion, dancing, giggling—but from my perch I saw something fascinating. Some kids at the party seemed to know only how to play a role. You could see it in their faces, in their body language, in their conversation. Their energy level was low, their conversation was stilted, and their faces were cold. They looked and acted bored. They weren't having fun.

But there were other kids who seemed to be totally comfortable with themselves. Their speech was gregarious, their smiles were authentic, and their conversation flowed. They were obviously having a lot of fun.

Watching all those young folks, I suddenly recalled an office that I used to work in. Some of the people there also seemed to be playing roles, staying within a narrow set of rules and boundaries, every word measured and calculated. They had very few ideas and little energy and joy; they had difficulty working with other people and achieved very poor results. But in that exact same office were others who were clearly being themselves. They tended to have endless ideas and an excitement in working together as teams. They were highly charged with energy and achieved amazing results.

When my thoughts returned to the party, I realized that the kids who weren't having any fun probably didn't trust themselves. They were afraid to express their thoughts or feelings because they weren't sure how others would react. I could easily imagine what kind of conversations went on in their families. But the kids who were real probably had parents who trusted them and taught them to trust themselves. They had a powerful reservoir of self-esteem; they could think for themselves and communicate their genuine feelings. Funny thing, I mused: The same thing goes for adults.

I firmly believe that without trust life can be very shallow. With trust barriers fall and life comes flooding in. Children remind us of that simple truth time and time again.

CHAPTER TEN
The Gift of Wisdom

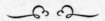

Smile Side Down
Corliss Brielman
Chicopee, Massachusetts

As I came down the stairs one morning, tons of laundry in my arms, tons of important business on my mind, I barely noticed my two-year-old daughter sitting on the couch. But there she stopped me with one question: "Mommy, why is your smile on upside down?"

Was I unhappy at that moment? No. Was I frowning? No. In her view my smile was on "upside down" because I was so preoccupied. Well, she made me laugh at myself and take notice of the truly important things all around us. To this day, fourteen years later, I still stop and wonder: Is my smile on upside down?

Children's simple wisdom helps us rid ourselves of the many distractions of adult thinking. They urge us to look at life with curiosity and wonder, without the clutter of "mind garbage" and preconceived notions. They remind us to switch our focus from the problems children seem to create to the far more important business of learning and growing together.

Little Red Socks
Mary Sheila Gall
McLean, Virginia

Another cold and rainy Sunday night. The laundry was piled in baskets by the door. The washer and dryer were across the open-air courtyard. Why did I always put it off until the last minute? I bundled Walter up in his little slicker and rain boots, and packed up his Golden Books and a toy truck.

As I searched for the detergent, I thought, I really don't want to do this. I *really* don't want to do this! But we were at the clean underwear crisis stage—with a week of school and work looming on the horizon. So we made several mad dashes across the courtyard to bring the baskets over. Not a soul in the laundry room! Hallelujah! I'd use three machines and get out of there in an hour—not bad at all—until I discovered only one machine was working. It would be a long night. As Walter and I sorted the colors and whites, we made up stories about castles and knights and dragons (mine) and He-Man, G.I. Joe, and micromachines (his).

Walter and I had been a family for only a few months. It seemed at times that the whole world opposed single-parent adoption and conspired to keep us apart with piles of paperwork and countless investigations and international battles. But God smiled on us and worked one of His miracles.

The adoption process was just the beginning. We both had so many adjustments to make. Walter learned English quickly and got into the swing of things in kindergarten. I was a slow learner. I was overpowered by my love for my son; it was immediate and all-consuming. But how to manage the everyday details of life? All those chores I had done routinely—work, bills, cleaning—now took a backseat to soccer and swings, reading *The Tale of Peter Rabbit* and baking cookies and making lemonade for the neighborhood kids running through our apartment.

That cold, rainy night had followed a busy day. I'd gotten up early that morning to wash the kitchen and bathroom floors. Later, Walter and I went to church—in the rain—and did the grocery shopping—in the rain. I cooked meals to freeze for the coming week, then stopped to read two chapters of *The Wind in the Willows* to Walter. As he took a nap, I tried to get through the paperwork on my desk, including immigration papers and medical insurance forms. Whoever designated Sunday as a day of rest wasn't a single parent! Supper finished, dishes washed, there was no putting it off any longer. On to the laundry.

Walter finally curled up on the laundry table with folded towels for a pillow. I was beginning to fade. It was late, and I was tired. One more load to go. The dryer groaned, did a shimmy shake, and died with my last load still in the washer. I burst into tears. But as I pulled the wet clothes out of the machine, I found a pair of little red socks. Those socks lifted my heart and put a smile on my face. Funny how the simplest things can help you focus on what is important.

I looked over at Walter—warm and snug and asleep—and I realized that laundry wasn't a measure of success or failure, or time management; it was just laundry. Our being a family and loving each other were the important things, and they were working just fine.

I woke Walter so that we could walk back to the apartment. It was still raining. He asked why we were bringing home clothes that were wet. As I explained about the dryer, his sunny disposition shone through. "Well," he said, "at least we won't have to worry about them getting wet in the rain, Mommy." And he was right.

Children remind us that the goal is not to find some final truth that will last for all time but instead to embrace the wisdom of the moment.

Grow Where You're Planted
Joan Rayford
Livonia, Michigan

We recently moved to a city that is considerably more expensive than where we used to live, so we had to rent an apartment rather than buy a house. One day when I started complaining about how I hated this place because I missed having my own yard and a garden, my eight-year-old son said that he liked it for exactly the same reasons.

"How can that be?" I asked.

"Because now that there's no lawn or garden," he replied, "you have more time to spend with us kids."

The Maze of the Unknown Potholes
Sheila Burns
Stehekin, Washington

The snow path to the house is becoming increasingly more exciting to walk on. Sierra and I were picking our routes this morning on the many paths that radiate from the house to where we park the truck out on the road. There is the low-hanging apple tree route that involves a great deal of ducking and face slapping and grumbling at the person who is walking ahead of you. There is the path made taboo thanks to the dog. There is an entire maze of paths filled with potholes punched in the snow by one of us unsuspecting snow walkers. And there is always the main path, which isn't so much in the mainstream of travel these days. It is riddled with nasty holes that are awaiting an opportunity to swallow an unsuspecting boot.

Sierra is bold and adventurous. She lifts her feet high and brings them down firmly with a satisfying crunch in the snow's crusts—direct denial that the snow is brittle and not likely to support even her slight frame. I am tentative. I don't lift my feet high, and I don't bring them down with any satisfying crunches. I am low-geared and go slow. I generally walk the shoulder of the main path. Sierra is courageous, and I am careful.

Sierra administers good advice to her cautious mom from her Maze of the Unknown Potholes. "It's not so bad if you keep your feet out of the holes that someone else has made," she says. This thought had crossed my mind, but I am busy trying to stay on top of the crust and not create any new holes. I murmur my thanks and keep picking my way.

"If I think 'light,' I don't fall in so easily." More excellent advice from this young sage, but her wonderful words of encouragement don't seem to help very much. I would love to please her by following her fine example, but I plunge through the crust on every other step. Sierra looks as if she is walking on terra firma. I look as if I am wading through two and a half feet of "quicksnow."

As we stomp and pick our respective ways, I see the contrast and realize that Sierra is still unafraid of falling. Sierra knows that if she does sink, she will simply pull herself out and stomp on, defying any new holes to open up and swallow her again. No great deliberation, no uncertainty. She moves with a sureness that I ascribe to youth and that I seem to lack.

I wonder what happened to my youthful confidence. At what point did it get buried under some layer of soggy, springtime snow? It makes me think of something I once read: "I wonder if one could tell the difference between flying and falling if there was nothing to crash into." Maybe I have made too many crash landings?

Our routes through life are diverse, but the destination is the same. Today it is home, sweet home. But I wonder about other destinations in my life. How am I going to move? Am I going to be perceptive enough to avoid the "holes" that others have made before me? And will I have enough faith to think "light" and be able to believe that I will stay on top of the path that I am traveling? And if I do fall, then I will have another lesson in understanding that there are things in life which are solid enough to crash into. I can't always be in a state of flying; my wings get tired, and a landing is inevitable.

Faith. Belief. Courage. It all seems to come down to choosing the path of least resistance. For me, anyway. And my choices seem to have a direct relationship to how much "extra" time I have on any given day. But what is life about (besides cold feet and wet boot liners)? Maybe it isn't possible to separate life into such simple categories. Maybe motherhood is the gift of a second shot at childhood. Not through the physical snow-stomping but going through life as Sierra does: She lifts her feet high and stomps with gusto.

I love Sierra's advice today. I hold it near and dear to my heart: "Think 'light.' Stay out of other people's potholes." I can do that. Maybe not every day, but it isn't an unworthy thing to set some days' sights on. There is enough loveliness and a lesson in all of the daily store of "things" that Sierra and I share together.

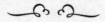

I ndeed, the wisdom of children so often shows us that life is a journey of ever-expanding opportunities about which path to take.

I'll Bring You Roses
Fran Simpson
Grand Junction, Colorado

My daughter, Pam, and I were pleased with the nursing home we had found for my husband, Richard, who was ill with Parkinson's disease. It was attractive and homey and offered the twenty-four-hour care he required. But as Richard was getting into the van that would transfer him to the new facility, a voice called out my name and a phone was handed to me. It was my daughter Kim who told me to keep Richard where he was. "Don't bring Dad over here. Keep him over there."

Hurrying back to the van, I told the driver that there was a problem and my husband could not be transferred. Richard was hastily helped into a wheelchair and taken to his old room. I found out what the problem was when Kim arrived. Earlier in the day Pam had gone to put my husband's furniture in his new room, which he was to share with a World War II veteran. She said that Captain X had spoken little. Then she and the captain had gone to the lobby to wait for Richard and me.

Kim and her daughter, Suki, arrived. As mother and daughter walked across the lobby toward Pam, Captain X sprang to his feet and, with his fists clenched, rushed toward the blond Kim. "Is she Japanese?" he shouted, pointing toward Suki.

Kim stopped, startled. "No, she's Korean."

"Is she your daughter?" he asked.

"Yes. She's adopted," Kim replied.

"I don't want to see her again!" the captain said, shaking his fist close to Kim's face.

Staff and onlookers were stunned, but nine-year-old Suki spoke up clearly. "My grandpa's coming to live here," she said. "We're waiting for him. The next time we come, I'll bring you roses."

For the first time the man looked at Suki's innocent face. Then, as suddenly as he had exploded in fury, he burst into tears and turned away to leave the room.

After he was gone, Pam, Kim, and the staff quickly agreed that the veteran's dementia made it impossible for my husband to be moved into that facility. But Suki had saved the day. I recalled the words of Isaiah 11:6: "A little child shall lead them."

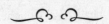

Suki had displayed simple wisdom. She knew that beneath the surface of the captain's anger was somebody who simply needed love. Her story reminded me of the following.

One afternoon I was hiking with Wister through the foothills near my home. Generally he walked close to me, but today, as we approached a small rise, a young fawn poked its head above the tall grass, and Wister was off like a shot. The fawn scrambled away, and the mother deer took off after Wister in a protective fury. I trailed farther and farther behind, my two human legs far from adequate to keep up with them.

For once, Wister completely ignored my whistling, calling, and shouting. Finally, the animals were out of sight, and I decided to save my breath for the run up a steep hill ahead. When I crested the hill, I saw Wister in the ravine below, his feet planted protectively around the cowering fawn. He was covering the little deer with big, slurpy dog kisses, his tail wagging in frenzied delight at his new friend. The doe stood quietly nearby, assured, I guess, that her baby was in no immediate danger.

Not so quiet or friendly, however, was an infuriated neighbor, who came yelling down the other side of the hill and grabbed Wister's collar to pull him away from the fawn.

"You irresponsible idiot," he shouted at me. "Why don't you have that dog on a leash? Don't you care about the wildlife around here?"

I watched, stunned, as the deer and her fawn scampered away.

"Take a good look at your dog, mister," the man continued, "because he's a dead dog. I ought to save the county pound the job. It's against the law to let a big dog run loose like that."

I snapped on Wister's leash. I was tempted to let this guy

really have it: "You jackass. Who the hell are you to tell me what to do? The dog is friendly. He wasn't hurting the deer." But suddenly I realized how valid his point of view was. Here was a man who genuinely cared about all life in this mountain paradise. I remembered the story of Suki and the captain, and instead of guns, I offered him "roses."

"Thank you for caring about the deer," I said quietly. "And it was irresponsible of me to let the dog run loose. I won't do that again."

With the dust settled, we began a conversation that continued at his kitchen table over cups of hot tea, with Wister curled up at our feet. What might have become a classic longtime Hatfield and McCoy feud changed in a few minutes to a rewarding friendship.

Even in the Midst of Adversity
April Morrison
Salem, Oregon

Like many eight-year-olds, my daughter, Alexandra, had been letting a lot of her responsibilities slide. She was neglecting her chores, skipping piano rehearsals and her Bible studies, and apparently abusing her public library privileges. She had lost another book.

We spent hours looking everywhere. We even searched her school library to see if it had been mistakenly returned there. Angry and frustrated, her father and I finally told Ali that she had just lost her privileges at both the public library and the school library for a month! Plus, she had to help pay for the book. We spent a major part of the morning lecturing her. She left for school with giant tears in her eyes.

Later that day as I was going through the monthly bills, I discovered that the public library had made a computer error on our book list. I quickly called the library and found that Ali had not lost the book after all. My husband and I felt terrible! I went to the store and bought two new books that I knew Ali would love. When we picked her up at school that afternoon, I explained the library's mistake and apologized—with giant tears in my eyes—for my anger that morning.

"Can you forgive me, Ali?" I asked. "Oh, sure, Mom!" she said, beaming with relief and happiness. "Because the way I see it, it's just like that guy in the Bible who had everything taken away. Remember Job? He lost all his money and his kids and his house, and he got real sick. But he never got mad at God, even though everyone said he should. And then in the end he got everything back—and even more! Just like me! The library is the most important thing in the world to me, and now I have all my privileges back and even more! Two new books. Wow!"

What did we do to deserve such a wise little girl?

When I Listen to Kids
John Crudele
Bloomington, Minnesota

Every year I have the privilege of speaking in several hundred elementary, junior, and senior high schools. I love working with kids! They are such honest mirrors to the world around them. In their actions and reactions, in what they say and don't say, children teach us, their teachers, how to reach them.

Somewhere along the way I learned that equal treatment of unequal learners is most unfair. All children come with a code, a key, or a password to unlock their hearts, minds, and souls. Children also give us all the clues we need to impact their lives forever. As every snowflake is different, so is every thumbprint. Every child leaves me with his or her own special memory, an insight to treasure for a lifetime. Are we totally present? Are we really listening? Do we honestly care?

Several years ago a fifth-grade boy was so excited to give me a poster he had made that he followed me into a rest room to make his presentation.

"Mister," he said.

"What can I do for you," I asked.

"I'd like to give you this poster that I made."

"What's your name?" I said.

"Aaron," he replied.

"Well, Aaron, I'm kind of busy right now," I said, which seemed like the appropriate response. "How about if you wait outside, and I'll get the poster from you in a second?"

"No!" he insisted. "Just turn around and I'll give you the poster."

If I turned around at that moment, I thought, we would both be in a world of trouble. So I said, "How about if you wait in the corner and you give me your poster in a moment?"

"Okay, but hurry," he said reluctantly.

Finally I turned around and said, "So now what's this poster you want to show me?"

He proudly unfolded a simple penciled proclamation. JUST SAY NO! was printed across the top, and underneath he had written a statement of deep, yet innocent insight and understanding: BE YOURSELF! Even at age ten Aaron knew that the hardest person in the world to be is what someone else wants you to be, and the easiest person in the world to be is yourself.

Since we both had each other's undivided attention, I thought this would be a good opportunity to find out what Aaron thought about his school. "Do you have any favorite teachers?" I asked.

"Sure I do," he replied.

"How can you tell? What makes them your favorite teachers?"

"Well . . ." He paused and then said matter-of-factly, "They ask me questions that I can answer."

That made sense, I thought. It sure beat having to respond to questions he couldn't answer. "What else?" I said with a puzzled look on my face.

"Well, they act like they really like me," Aaron said kind of sheepishly.

"Do you mean they don't have to really like you? They can just act like it?" I asked.

"No!" he said with exasperation. "I can tell if they really like me."

"You seem as though you'd be easy to like," I said.

He grinned, spun an about-face, and ran off to his next class.

As I walked off to teach my next lesson, I reflected on the one I had just learned. Aaron had given me so much more than a poster. "Make sure the students can tell that you really like them, that you care!"

There is no way we can overestimate the effect we have on others. We are never on the path of life alone. Every action we take, every smile we smile, every word we utter is a statement about the value of the person who is walking beside us. And from there the actions, the smiles, and the words ripple out forever.

Every moment we are true to ourselves, we offer even more value to others. A recent incident reminded me of that, all too painfully.

From lending my book to a stranger on a plane to answering a question on the phone or keynoting a national conference, I look at each situation equally—as an opportunity to help children and families. At least I did until I was booked by The Young Presidents Organization, an international organization made up of presidents and CEOs of major corporations.

As soon as the booking was confirmed, I began to dream

about the potential for meaningful family and community change. These influential leaders would take my message back to their employees, their families, and their communities, thus helping millions of children. This was not a normal assignment, I kept thinking. This one was special.

This particular booking carried an even greater meaning because the venue was a father-daughter outdoor adventure camp retreat. Ali and I would spend three days together tackling everything from rope courses to canoeing.

We arrived at the camp and began our outdoor activities with great enthusiasm, pausing during the heat of each day while I conducted a brief seminar on my 10 Greatest Gifts program. But something was out of sync. I wasn't flowing naturally, either outside with Ali or inside as a speaker. I had to think about every sentence. I had to work hard to remember the presentation points and stories, and I felt forced and contrived during every conversation. I wasn't having a lick of fun. In our eight-man bunkhouse I felt like a black sheep. For some reason I was having a very hard time fitting in.

To make matters even worse, the responses I was getting were not typical at all. Some of the YPOers were enthusiastic and saw ways in which they could help people in their communities, but others were lukewarm at best. By now I was spending a considerable amount of time trying to figure out why I wasn't able to reach them.

Ali noticed my discomfort, and as we were loading the car to leave, she asked me what was wrong. I acknowledged that things hadn't gone very well, but I didn't know why. I asked her if she had any ideas.

"Sure do," she said, her eyes sparkling with love and innocent truth. "Daddy, you were just not being yourself."

She was right, I realized. I hadn't been myself at all. I'd

been trying to be a YPOer. I had been a young executive and president of my own company years ago. Now I'd been trying to play the role of somebody I no longer was, and since that person wasn't really me, there wasn't much depth to the person I was playing. Because I had given up everything that made me unique, I had very little to give and share.

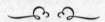

The YPOers were a wonderful group. They were immensely successful in their careers, and they hadn't achieved that level of success without many other fine attributes. Most of them had interesting things to share and discuss, and cared about their families and communities. They had treated me well, but I just hadn't treated myself well.

Ali taught me that I don't have to fit myself into someone else's rating scale. I don't have to compare myself to anyone else or pretend to be someone I'm not. That can only be a losing battle since we can always find someone more experienced and skilled than we are in any given field. Instead, we can decide how we're going to rate ourselves on our own scale. We can choose an internal rating system or an external one. We can rate ourselves on our own qualities and efforts.

I know that when I nurture my own strengths and skills and passions, I have so much more to contribute. It's a simple reality of life. When I focus on my strengths, I have something I can manage and build on. When I focus on my weaknesses, they become self-perpetuating and unmanageable. As I continue to evolve and grow, my most important job, as I discovered through Ali, is to learn to be myself.

Not Even God Can Stop You
Pamela Larson
Regina, Saskatchewan

At the start of my recovery from an alcohol/drug addiction, I had little faith and not enough self-esteem to believe that my sons and I deserved a good life. Driving home from visiting my family at Easter on a lovely spring evening in 1982, I was feeling more alienated from them than when I was actively drinking. They didn't—or wouldn't—accept the fact that I had a problem.

I appealed to my seven-year-old son, Shawn. "I've prayed to God about helping me to stop drinking, and He told me that if it's what makes me feel better, do it. Even He doesn't care."

Tears came to Shawn's eyes. "Mom, not even God can stop you from drinking if you don't want His help. That's your choice."

And my choice has been never to drink again, thanks to that awakening.

I Have Always Believed
Rev. Kathleen Bostrom
Wildwood, Illinois

In the early years of our ministry, prior to the arrival of our own children, Greg and I loved to ask the kids open-ended questions during the children's time in worship. We could always count on a few outgoing, verbal tykes to speak up and say anything that came to mind. We could also identify the parents of these loquacious youngsters by the way they would sink down in the pew, shake their blushing faces, or laughingly bury their heads in their hands.

"Just you wait!" they would tell us gleefully. "Someday it will be your children up front, and then we can watch you squirm!"

This prophecy came to pass. Our three children were born within four years and were welcomed with much love on the part of the whole congregation. It wasn't long before Christopher, the oldest, joined the rest of the younger folks on the steps of the chancel, delighting one and all as he spontaneously gave Greg and me an affectionate hug after the closing prayer. He always had something to say, relevant or not. The parents who had suffered through their own children's orations a few years before now sat smugly in the pews, grinning with amusement as we tried to keep our young son in check.

One Sunday morning during the children's time, Greg was explaining the proximity of God. "Where is God?" he asked the kids. "Is God in this church? Is God in the sky?"

Several children raised their hands with suggestions. Then it was Christopher's turn. His hand lifted high, he would not lower it until Greg reluctantly called his name.

Christopher looked up at his father, his brown velvet eyes seeing beyond time and place. "I have always believed," he said with the accumulated knowledge of a five-year-old and all the wisdom of the ages, "that the whole world was in God's heart."

The church was hushed. "Let us pray," Greg said, and we all bowed our heads. Nothing else needed to be said.

CHAPTER ELEVEN
The Gift of Courage

—⟨❦⟩—

When Prayers Are Answered
Kevin Connolly
Richmond, Virginia

I would never have imagined that one of the most influential people in my life would be a twelve-year-old girl. I met Melissa when I was a pediatric resident. She had leukemia and was frequently in the hospital. Despite her illness she always had a bright outlook and continually demonstrated how you can change a situation by changing your attitude toward it.

When chemotherapy caused her hair to fall out, Melissa bought a long-haired brown wig. She would put her clothes on backward and turn the wig around to cover her face. Then she would draw a face on the back of her bald head and sit in the hospital hallways to get a laugh.

Once, a nurse handed Melissa a specimen cup and asked for a urine sample. She later returned to find Melissa sitting in bed, the cup filled with the amber liquid. As the nurse started to take the cup, Melissa said, "No, wait! I want it back!" She took the cup and drank the liquid. The nurse stood aghast, and Melissa laughed hysterically. She had filled the cup with apple juice.

Though a child, she lived passionately. While most terminally ill children visit Disney World through the Make-A-Wish Foundation, Melissa went to Space Camp to train as an astronaut. She was wise beyond her years and taught me a lesson that will live forever in my heart.

One spring day, while I had free time between seeing patients, Melissa came down the hall from her routine clinic visit. We sat and talked about how she was feeling. She had been through all the routine treatments, but her leukemia raged on. Her only chance for survival was a bone marrow transplant, but unfortunately a perfectly compatible match could not be found. Most medical centers therefore refused to attempt this treatment, but despite the poor odds of success, a children's hospital in Minnesota had agreed to try the procedure.

As we sat there talking about her future, I asked Melissa if she was scared.

"Yeah, a little," she said. "It's not a perfect match, but it's the best chance I have. What else can I do but pray?"

"Well, I'm praying for you, too." I said. "I hope our prayers are answered."

"Oh, they will be," Melissa said, her gaze drifting out the window and up into the blue sky. "God answers all prayers." She paused and then added, "But sometimes the answer is no."

Melissa died two months later.

Children often teach us what courage really means. They don't blame or justify but instead accept the reality of their situation and keep on going. What if we could all be like that? Fear is a normal part of life, but any fear that we choose not to face can literally take over our lives. All progress comes to a dead stop.

My daughter, Emmy, reminded me how important it is to work through fear.

One weekend we were rock climbing in Eldorado Canyon outside Boulder, Colorado. It wasn't an easy climb, and

Emmy was trembling with fear at many of the moves she was required to make.

"How do I use this carbineer?" she would ask our coach, Rick. "Which foothold is the best one here?" Then she would inch up the rock face and pose yet another question.

Emmy's apprehension could easily have stopped her at any moment, yet she kept climbing, stretching, pushing her limits into this new territory. Suddenly her fear seemed to dissolve as she reached the top of a rock face. "It's okay to be afraid," she nearly shouted to me, "but it's not okay to be afraid to be afraid."

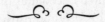

When we let ourselves be consumed by fear, everything we attempt is doomed to failure. Life can be just as difficult as climbing a mountain. It takes courage, and kids teach us that courage doesn't mean we know all the answers. To be courageous means to be vulnerable, to ask if we don't know, to be who we really are and be willing to take one more little step into that unknown void called life.

Ask Not What He Cannot Do
Lucy Beale
Denver, Colorado

When Brian was first diagnosed with cerebral palsy, I worried about what would become of him. Would he ever ride a bike or play tennis or even walk? It took me a while to know that the right question was: "What will this child make of himself?" As he grew and conquered his life's challenges, I wanted to think that Brian got his inspiration from me or from his dad. But, in truth, his successes and attitudes came from within his own soul and spirit.

I once asked him why he did all the things he did, such as make the honor roll consistently, play basketball, become an Eagle Scout, and earn yet another belt in tae kwon do. "Mom, for the accomplishment," he replied. When I asked for clarification, he repeated, "Mom, for the accomplishment."

But then it came time to learn how to drive. He got his permit at fifteen years nine months and passed his test at age nineteen years three months. It took him three and a half years to learn to drive a car. Now, any teenage boy will probably do whatever it takes to learn to drive and get his "wheels," but for Brian it was an extraordinary accomplishment.

Fortunately, one of his driving instructors took Brian under his wing and made him his "project." They drove together for several months. It took months and months of eye therapy for Brian to develop his peripheral vision; he spent hours tracing large infinity symbols in the air and tracking them with his eyes. He did his exercises faithfully.

Brian never seemed discouraged. On a single day he flunked his driver's test twice. The message on my voice mail simply stated, "Mom, I failed my driver's test two times today. Mom, I am disappointed." That was all. He didn't beat himself up. He didn't cry or fuss or swear or act out. He kept learning.

Many teachers wondered why Brian scored so high on standardized tests, given his IQ. They finally realized that it was because for him every question was a new question. He didn't base his answers on whether he thought he had answered the prior question correctly or not, as most of us do. For Brian, every day is a new day. Every question is a brand-new question. Every driver's test is a brand-new test. He didn't believe he couldn't.

One evening he and I were having dinner at our favorite sushi place. "You know, Brian," I reminded him, "you might not go to college because of your disabilities." I did not want him to have his heart set on it. He listened, heard me, and didn't say anything. In fact, he changed the subject.

Twenty minutes later, though, he said, "Mom, remember when they said I might never walk or be able to ride a bike or run?" He held out his hands as if to accentuate his body and his inner brilliance. "Mom, look at me now."

That was all he said about college that night, and it was all he needed to say. I got the message. Far be it from me to tell him what he cannot do. I decided in that moment that I would never again attempt to limit anyone's capabilities, including my own. Accomplishment has nothing to do with capability and everything to do with inner light and desire. It has to do with inner fire or, as Brian says, " 'Nike-ing' it, Mom."

He finally passed his driver's test and got a car. It has given him the freedom and feeling of manhood he so richly desired and deserved. And I know just how he'll turn out—because he already has.

Like many of us, I grew up thinking that making mistakes was bad and that I had to work for a grade rather than an answer. Children have shown me that we can keep trying and that we often learn best through our mistakes. What would it be like if we all learned to take risks rather than shut down, to judge others on intent not outcome, to put forth a one-hundred-percent effort even when success is not assured?

When Ali was scared about a new challenge, she would first become quiet and thoughtful. Then expressions of both fear and courage chased each other across her face. And when finally she walked through the fear and met the challenge, her expression was a mixture of pride and pure delight. Even though fear can be so paralyzing to some people, Ali almost always had the courage to take the next step.

It was the first day of the University of Colorado's girls'

basketball camp, and Ali had asked me to walk with her to the area where 150 other girls were warming up. As we stood at the entrance to the gym, her damp hand clung to mine. She watched the girls dribbling and shooting while I watched that familiar range of emotions play across her face.

"Okay, Dad, you can go now," she said a few minutes later. She trotted out on the court and began retrieving balls. I could still see that look of fear and courage on her face—but once again she was pushing through. The next day when we arrived to pick her up, Emmy and I noticed a great improvement in Ali's confidence and courage. And by the third day she was clearly having fun.

The coaches announced that they would be awarding trophies on the final day to the girl on each team who had tried the hardest and improved the most, ten trophies in all. But when Emmy and I walked into the gym that day to pick up Ali, they had already given the trophies to the girls on two of the teams, including Ali's. "I bet Ali won the trophy on her team!" Emmy said.

After the remaining trophies had been awarded, Emmy ran off to find her sister and emerged from the crowd two minutes later. "Ali won the trophy. Ali won the trophy!" she shouted, jumping up and down with excitement. When Ali finally appeared with her trophy, the look on her face was priceless. I wished I could bottle it up and bring it out whenever I needed a shot of courage.

I've found that many parents stifle their kids' ability to learn from their mistakes by insisting they do it right or not at all. Or their attitude is that it's okay to walk away from something rather than face one's fears about it. Or they do not emphasize the immense pride in doing one's very best even though you may not be the best.

I received another gift that day at the gym, a gift that touched me deeply (although that didn't sink in until later). It came from Emmy. I have never seen a child so genuinely happy for another. She wasn't envious, she wasn't jealous, she wasn't comparing herself to Ali. She was simply ecstatic for her sister's success. She knew there were plenty of successes to go around and that her sister's triumph did not in any way detract from her. What would the world be like if we all felt like that?

A Handful of Band-Aids
Janine Morales
Fresno, California

Two sparkling eyes peered into my hospital room and in a flash were gone. Down the hall I could hear giggling. This was, after all, a children's hospital. Although I was almost twenty-two years old, I still went to Valley Children's Hospital because of the uniqueness of a stomach disorder I'd had since I was an infant. My head was pounding as I lay back to rest.

Later in the afternoon a tiny figure appeared next to my bed. "Here," she said. She placed something in my hand and was gone. I examined what she had given me: a handful of new "Lion King" Band-Aids. When the nurse came in to check my IV, she saw the Band-Aids. "I see Kayla's been here to visit," she said, smiling.

Around 7:30 P.M. that same day while my mom was visiting me, the eyes reappeared at my door. "Hi, Kayla," I said. "Why don't you come in?"

She entered the room slowly, looked around, and sat down on the footstool of a big chair. My mom and I were delighted with her company. Suddenly she announced, "I want to be in your room."

"Gosh, Kayla, that would be great, but I already have a roommate," I replied. Her huge eyes scanned the tiny room. "It's okay, I don't need much room. I can stay right here," she said, patting the footstool. I wasn't quite sure how to answer, but before I could, she was off running down the hall, only to reappear a few minutes later toting a huge gift bag. Oh, no, I thought. She *is* moving in!

One by one three-year-old Kayla produced treasure after treasure from the bag. First came a box of scented marking pens. She carefully opened each one, smelled it, then held it for me to smell. I replaced the cap and returned each one equally as carefully to its place in the box.

Kayla noticed a man on the television with long unruly hair and a full beard. "Oh, my, look at that hair," my mom said from the other side of the room. Kayla looked at me. "I don't have any hair," she confessed. Before anyone could react, she declared, "But it's okay."

"You're right," I said. "It doesn't matter. You have a cute head." She giggled and turned her attention once more to her bag. Now she retrieved sticker after sticker from her treasures and with great intensity began decorating my long white hospital gown. She must have placed at least one hundred stickers on the front and all along each arm of my gown, and when she was finished, she stood admiring her work. "There, Janine, now you are pretty," she said. "You were too plain before."

When her nurse arrived to announce that it was time for her to return to her room for her chemotherapy, Kayla collected her treasures, started out of the room, then stopped. She climbed on my bed to give me a hug. "I love you, Janine. Can I come back tomorrow?"

"Of course you can. I'll be waiting for you."

Chemotherapy may have taken Kayla's hair, but she was full of love and spirit and courage. Modern medicine has made many advances in treatment for my condition, but that night a few scented pens, a handful of Band-Aids, and millions of stickers did more for me than any medical treatment could.

CHAPTER TWELVE

The Gift of Acceptance

~—⚬3 ⚬2—~

Someone Will Bloom
Patricia Mahar Simpson
Princeton, New Jersey

The greatest gift I ever received from a child was actually given to me by three children, triplets: Andrew, Emily, and Amy. Simply being their mother and witnessing their joy in life and their natural wisdom is a gift that I experience, often with amazement, each day. But the most important insight they have given me to date occurred when they were seven years old, although the experiences leading up to it had been ongoing for several years.

Every year in school my daughter Emily, a bright, happy, and sociable child, has been the recipient of unusual friendships. Adults might describe these friends as "difficult" children. Their teachers might describe them as "challenging" students. In kindergarten it was a little boy named Quentin who was full of energy and often found it difficult to participate appropriately in class. For some unknown reason he began playing with Emily, and over the course of the year his behavior and his ability to participate in class improved dramatically, particularly when she was nearby. On the last day of school that year, Quentin gave both Emily and the teacher a long-stemmed, ribbon-tied rose. Emily's expression of pure pleasure and innocent amazement when she showed me the rose was one I will never forget.

In first grade the unusual friendship, with the same positive outcome, happened with a different child (Quentin had moved away over the summer). And in second grade it happened yet again. I was unaware of this new friendship until I heard my children talking about John. We had moved to a new town and the children were in a new school, so there were many children I had yet to meet. After listening to them, I wondered a little about this unlikely friendship. What in the world did Emily have in common with a boy who seemed to be in trouble so often?

Their teachers frequently commented on the calming effect that Emily had on John, and they often put the two children together to work on team projects. We adults wondered among ourselves about how Emily was able to trigger the positive behavior, a goal that others had attempted without success.

Toward the end of the school year, on a warm day in late spring, Amy, Andrew, Emily, and I were in the car on our way from school to piano lessons. As usual the kids were in the backseat chattering away, sharing the news of the day. Since they are all in the same grade, they often play with the same friends and have recess and lunch at the same time. On this day they were discussing important playground events, and John's name came up. I used the opportunity to ask (in what I thought was a rather offhand way), "Emily, why do you think John behaves so much better when he's around you?"

"I don't know, Mom," she said, shrugging her shoulders. Emily has never found much use for introspection, and she clearly didn't see a need to begin now. Not ready to give up, I asked Amy and Andrew if they had any ideas. In the rearview mirror I could see Amy's sweet face as she pondered this question. It was then that Andrew, my wise, wacky, and wonderful son, gave me the answer.

"She's John's ant, Mom," he said.

"Aunt?" I asked, wondering what in the world he meant. "How could she possibly be his aunt?"

"You know, Mom, like an ant on a flower that chews off the outer part so the flower can bloom. Emily helps John bloom."

I was amazed. This from Andrew, king of G.I. Joe, whose favorite movie was *Star Wars* and whose favorite book was *The Story of D-day*. On the other hand, I thought to myself, this is the same boy who stopped by almost every day after school to visit with our seventy-something neighbor, Mrs. Churchill, sharing stories, smiles, and doughnuts.

And that was it—wisdom from a seven-year-old. Be a friend without judging or manipulating or trying to improve someone. Be an ant and someone will bloom.

"Do you get it, Mom?" the three of them asked more or less simultaneously.

I got it.

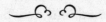

Acceptance seems to come easily to children, but it's a lesson I've been trying to learn for years. Perhaps because I used to own a talent agency—a business that often judges people primarily on their appearance—I have a tendency to see the surface of people; kids see what's inside. They don't see color or income or career track or neighborhood status—at least not until we teach them to.

Cool Pizza
Rob and Maureen Bennett
Grosse Pointe Woods, Michigan

The owner of Little Caesars Pizza also owns the Detroit Tigers, the professional baseball club. I work for Little Caesars in the risk management department and deal with the Tigers on a routine basis. One day I was able to get a team-autographed baseball, which I gave to my five-year-old son, Jimmy. I was pretty happy with myself, thinking I had been able to get him a very special gift that most kids would love to have.

The next day Jimmy was playing with a friend in his room when my wife overheard his friend ask, "What's this ball with all the writing on it?"

"I don't know," Jimmy answered. "It's a bunch of pizza guys who work with my dad."

"Your dad makes pizza?" his friend crowed. "That's cool!"

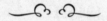

The things that impress kids often surprise us. The people they choose for friends—both grown-ups and other kids—can sometimes be surprising, too. But instead of criticizing them or trying to force our preferences and prejudices on them, we would do better to try to see things through their eyes and to be as accepting as they are.

Blooming One Long Day at a Time
Lucy Beale
Denver, Colorado

By the time Brian was six months old, I knew something was not quite right. He was my first, only, and much desired child. Big happy blue eyes and reddish-blond hair, but he hadn't yet crawled or sat or even tried to. He rolled as a way to explore, and he smiled. Or else he fussed softly and frequently. Finally, by the time he was a year old, I had managed to convince his pediatrician that something was wrong. Brian still only rolled and smiled. The doctor agreed to tests "to make me feel better."

The results? Cerebral palsy. Perhaps Brian could learn to

walk, but he would probably never ride a bike or play ball. In other words, they really did not know.

Brian walked by the time he was two. That whole year we went to walking therapy three times every week and practiced for as long as both he and I could tolerate at a time.

By two and a half years everything that could be tested wasn't quite right. He couldn't talk or eat correctly. He was highly allergic to almost everything one could reasonably purchase in the grocery store. The ear infections he had suffered since he was nine months were still rampant. He had returned to walking therapy because a foot hadn't turned correctly. He was in occupational therapy three times a week in addition to ever-constant speech therapy. He also needed seven operations, mostly for his ear infections.

I stitched many needlepoint pillows in hospital waiting rooms. I cooked rather peculiar foods, hoping that he wouldn't react to them and become so hyperactive that I couldn't handle him. The special foods seemed to make little difference, however. He was so hypersensitive to everything that he was constantly racing around.

I was a mentally, emotionally, and physically tired and discouraged mother. None of why this had happened made any sense. There were no answers. Not one of the experts could really make it better. No "miracles" were happening. It was one day at a time, one long day at a time.

I ate compulsively. And cried. And complained. I felt sorry for myself and resented my plight, as well as Brian's. By the age of three and a half he was becoming a behavior problem. And so was I. Learning had come easy to me, and so had academic accomplishments. I thought I was a failure.

About this time I enrolled Brian in a toddlers' gymnastics class. During one class the teacher instructed all of the children to sit down in a circle. One little girl stood outside the circle crying. Brian rushed up to her, hugged her, and began to comfort her—that is, until the teacher yelled at him to let her cry and get himself into that circle. I studied the situation for a moment. What Brian had been scolded for was the appropriate thing to do, wasn't it? To comfort someone in need. To gently draw the frightened child back into the circle rather than to exclude her and just let her cry.

Brian had a comprehension and compassion that I had caught glimpses of from time to time. Observing him opened a possibility to me that perhaps I could be more sympathetic about his situation. But the unanswered question was how. And then one day, as I was figuring out what to cook for dinner, feeling very sorry for myself and practically in tears, I said, "God help me. This is awful." Then what I can only call a miracle occurred. It transformed how I thought and felt and how I regarded my son. In that moment he became the beautiful being he had always been, a boy I had been unable to see. He took his rightful place as my perfect teacher.

"Oh, my gosh," I said to myself. "I have been looking at this incorrectly. I have been thinking that there is something wrong with Brian. The problem is that there is something wrong with the way I have been perceiving him."

Then I made a declaration of this truth to myself and to the universe: "There is absolutely nothing wrong with this child. He is merely different from other children. He is like a different kind of rosebush that takes different nurturing to blossom and bloom. I have been hiring therapists and doctors who also think there is something wrong with Brian. We've all been trying to 'fix' him, and I am through with this. From now on I will hire only those professionals who share my new point of view."

The next day I went page by page through the phone book seeking out professionals who would work with Brian the way I wanted and treat both of us with dignity. It didn't take long before a brilliant speech therapist came our way who did not expect a hyperactive child to sit still for therapy, a pediatrician who believed me when I said Brian was highly allergic to so many foods, and a preschool that had teachers who could enjoy him rather than see him as a discipline problem.

That moment changed my life, to say nothing of Brian's. I learned that all of life is perception, that I can choose to see people as okay the way they are, or not. I discovered that by changing my perception, I can change absolutely anything. In that flash I acquired years and years of wisdom and patience, understanding and compassion.

Brian gave me the gift of true perception, and he has given that same gift to his teachers and friends and others through his belief in himself, his kindness, his accomplishments, and through his spirit. Today, Brian is nineteen and will be graduating from high school soon. He has played on the basketball team and been on the honor roll consistently. He's an Eagle Scout and has practiced tae kwon do for more than ten years.

Funny how things come full circle. Several months ago I was once again in the car in the Children's Hospital parking lot, waiting for Brian. But it was the first time I had ever been there without his needing an operation or speech or occupational therapy. For, you see, Brian has chosen to devote his foreseeable future to working with sick children and is volunteering at the hospital. I cry in joy now at the beauty of this child who just needed to blossom and bloom in a different way.

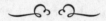

When we don't accept people for who they are and try to change them, we usually end up in a snarled web of wasted energy. They become defensive trying to justify themselves or take the offensive and criticize us. Putting labels on people who are somehow different from us is also self-defeating, keeping us in old, usually destructive patterns. I can't imagine living in a world where everyone was exactly the same.

She Did It Her Way
Kathy DeVaughn
Richmond, Virginia

Mama always said that Rachel was "the lazy one" of us four girls. And at ages four, six, seven, and eight, we believed everything Mama said. Naturally we accepted her assessment of us and her labels. Whenever Rachel didn't do something we wanted her to do, we chalked it up to her being lazy. But looking back on it now, nearly forty years later, I can see that none of us had a clue about Rachel's emerging personality.

At six I viewed four-year-old Rachel as a personal challenge. Despite her apparently low energy level, I believed that I could engage her in my idea of fun. Oh, sure, she thought she preferred to rock quietly in a chair while sucking her finger, with the radio playing in the background, but I would show her what real fun was.

I had started school and loved everything about it. Having found the keys to paradise, I was determined that Rachel should experience it, too, whether she wanted to or not. Every day I'd come home from school and insist on teaching her what I'd learned. But she had other ideas and would run and hide, getting away from me whenever she could. I persevered, though, and before long Rachel knew the songs and stories I had learned. I even had this reluctant four-year-old reading from one of my schoolbooks. Remarkable!

One day a storm knocked out our electricity. Mama was afraid of storms, and she absolutely forbade any loud noises or horsing around when it was stormy. So we four girls usually made up stories to tell each other or used a flashlight to cast finger shadows on the wall. On this day I decided to show off Rachel's reading. She didn't want to do it—she was having too much fun sucking that finger and rocking and humming to herself—but we all made such a fuss that she finally gave in. I ran and got the book, and little Rachel read and read by the light coming through the window.

Mama and my sisters were exclaiming over this amazing accomplishment when suddenly the lights blinked back on. Feeling proud, I aimed a big smile at Rachel, who was still "reading" —from a book she was holding upside down.

Now in our forties, my sisters and I have come to know Rachel better. We are well acquainted with that aspect of her personality that spends minimal energy on things she doesn't really want to do, while approaching them in her own way. She has taught us all a lesson about individual values. If I had learned Rachel's lesson and accepted it back then, it would've saved me a lot of trouble over the years. But for a long time I just didn't get it.

My daughter Emmy reminded me that welcoming someone means giving our acceptance wholeheartedly even though they may seem closed to our love.

It happened on a Friday. The fourth graders were picking their new project teams, and nobody wanted Cathy. She had been in Emmy's fourth-grade class for only two weeks, and it had not been easy for anyone. First of all, there was the communication barrier. Cathy spoke only a few words of English, and no one in this affluent community of five thousand spoke Chinese. Furthermore, Cathy's clothes were covered with stains and holes, and her hair was filthy. It was common knowledge that she didn't have a mom and her dad was a dishwasher at a local restaurant. They lived with several other siblings in a tacky boardinghouse on the edge of town. Cathy was already accustomed to being shunned and ridiculed by most of the children.

Now, at two o'clock on Friday afternoon, the team selection process was nearly complete, and not a single person had been willing to look at Cathy—until it was Emmy's turn. The room fell silent as she softly called out Cathy's name. Emmy's teammates flashed their discomfort. Cathy sat frozen, her eyes turned down to her desk. Emmy's gaze was steady and determined as she walked across the room to Cathy's desk, took her by the hand, and led her to the team.

A few days later Emmy asked Cathy if they could study together. "No," Cathy said abruptly.

Emmy asked again the next day. No, again.

Could she teach her some Chinese words? Emmy asked. At last some common ground. Cathy said yes. A few days later, however, Emmy tried to give Cathy a little present, but she refused to take it. Undaunted, Emmy simply begin to play with Cathy on the playground and gave her the present two weeks later.

Emmy's first two invitations to Cathy to come over on Saturday to play were turned down. When she finally said yes, Emmy's mother was surprised that Cathy and Emmy hardly knew any common words. But it didn't matter. Barbie dolls enchanted them for hours; they played hide-and-seek all over the house and yard; they jumped on the bed, ate frosting, and even did their homework together. Emmy's mother sent Cathy home that day with some extra clothing, but everything was promptly returned by Cathy's father.

After many Saturdays playing with Emmy and learning hundreds of words between them, Cathy suddenly disappeared. No calls and no letters. The tenants at their boardinghouse said that Cathy and her family had moved away in the night and left no forwarding address.

Emmy didn't say much, but I could tell she was worried. I was afraid to encourage her to hope for a letter, because I wasn't sure how Cathy felt about her. I had never seen Cathy or her dad invite Emmy over or show much outward friendship. Then about a week later there was a letter in the mailbox addressed to Emmy in a child's handwriting.

der eme we move to dnver. I like you rite to me. I mis you. Bes frends forever.

As Emmy ran off to write her first letter to Cathy, I pondered the gifts these children had shared. Until now I had pretty much watched Cathy from a distance. "That's nice," I thought. "What sweet children." Now I realized that Emmy had given me a lesson in acceptance and true friendship that would last a lifetime.

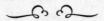

I don't think Emmy lost any of her old friends because of her friendship with Cathy, and I don't think she would have cared if she had. Her heart was simply set on doing what was right and on accepting another human being. She had the courage to act on her convictions. In the process, the girls became lasting friends and learned a lot about each other's language and customs.

The Unpretentious
Sande Snead Fulk
Colonial Heights, Virginia

Because my husband's family lives in San Diego and we live outside of Richmond, Virginia, we don't get to see them very often. Our annual or semiannual visits to them are a bit stressful for me because I want them to go well. I want everything to be just right, so the children are primed for weeks or even months about behavior and manners, which they should have been learning all along, of course, but I seem to give them a crash course right before our visits out west.

Also, I carefully select their best clothes for the trip, and sometimes even buy a few new things such as shoes and tights to make the best possible impression. At six, my oldest child, Brittany, is quite amused by all these preparations. She has never been one to try to impress anyone. When most other children are saying, "Hey, Mom! Look at me! Watch me do this," Brittany is more likely to slip away and quietly succeed in her own achievements, like going off the diving board at age four or reading at a second-grade level at age five.

Now that she is in kindergarten, I send her off to school in a freshly pressed dress with matching socks and shoes, and always with a bow in her squeaky clean hair. Invariably, she comes home with shoes on the wrong feet, no socks, no bow, and a vest or belt missing from the outfit she was wearing.

Nevertheless, I continue to strive for neatness, cleanliness, and matching little-girl outfits for Brittany and her sister, Nicole, who is three. Imagine how pleased I was when my mother gave them matching winter coats and hats for Christmas 1993 before our trip to San Diego. They are beautiful. Brittany's coat is red wool with black velvet trim, and the black velvet hat has a red plaid band. Nicole's coat is turquoise blue wool with black velvet trim, with a matching hat.

I wanted them to look like perfect little ladies for their grandparents who had not seen them for a long time. For the plane ride they wore dresses and white tights with black patent leather shoes. They might have been a bit uncomfortable on the six-hour flight, but by gosh they looked good.

It was about seventy-five or eighty degrees when we got off the plane in San Diego, but I had lugged those beautiful winter coats all the way across the country and by golly they would be wearing those coats when they greeted their grandparents.

Before we got off the plane, I nervously began to fuss with their clothes, pulling up tights and adjusting their hair bows.

Next I tried putting their coats on, but Brittany, then four, balked. "Come on, Brittany," I pleaded. "I want Gammer and PaPa to see how pretty you look in your new coats."

"We're pretty without our new coats," she said.

I kept pleading with her, telling her that I wanted her to look nice and how Gammer would say, "Oh, what lovely coats."

"Mom," she said with a child's innocence and honesty, "Gammer will be looking at us, not our coats." She was right, of course. Not another word was said about those nice new coats.

I continue to learn this lesson every day: What is on the outside really doesn't matter. It's what's on the inside that is so important.

Brittany seems to gravitate toward children who appear to me to be dirty and unkempt looking. But invariably I find that these children who may not be too well put together on the outside are really pretty neat kids on the inside. I wonder how many friends I may have passed by because they didn't meet my strict standards for attractiveness.

Children cut through the fluff and get right to the heart of the matter. They can find kindred spirits dressed in any clothing because, unlike adults, they are not blinded by the packaging.

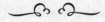

Adults often see things in black and white, good and bad, acceptable and unacceptable. More tolerant and forgiving, kids don't draw such sharp distinctions. Sometimes acceptance can be as simple as a kiss.

Touched by a Hidden Love
Eric Davenport
Rexburg, Idaho

My therapy session with Elizabeth was over. She is a delightful four-year-old child who has a neurological disorder called autism. As always, I was reluctant to leave her, but it had been a rough day and I was anxious to get home. As I turned to walk to the door, I heard the rustling of a diaper along with the squeak of an old high chair. I turned around to catch a glimpse of Elizabeth's familiar face before I went home. She was kneeling quietly, with her hands gripping the faded wooden bars of her chair. With a cheerful look on her face that matched her pink-and-white summer dress, she peered over the back rest of the chair like a child peeking over a fence.

The warmth of Elizabeth's smile had always been an invitation that brought me back to her home as a volunteer every Saturday afternoon. I noticed her dark brown eyes and reflected on the many happy moments we'd spent together. Wagon trips up and down her street delighted both of us. Her fingers bounced, painting gentle shadows on the pavement as I sang, "No more monkeys jumpin' on the bed." As the cadence of children's songs continued down the block, I'd pull her in tight circles. Round and round we'd go, her endless giggle blending with the bumping of the wagon wheels against the empty street. Those were the moments I would never forget. Moments like that.

As I turned to tell her good-bye that afternoon, I had to laugh at the sight of her. She had just finished a green salad with ranch dressing that now covered her face. I bent over to give her a kiss, another weekly routine, but I tried to avoid the mess by planting the kiss on her cheek. Satisfied, I stepped back to get her approval, but it wasn't there. It seemed that Elizabeth's family had taught her about kisses and where they belonged. She looked at me in confusion as if to say, "Dummy, don't you know where kisses go?"

I chuckled when I realized what I had to do. My eyes began to squint as I approached her face. The smell of ranch dressing tickled my nose as I got even closer. Then smack! More like slop! I quickly pulled back to wipe the gunk off my face. "Yuck!" I told her with a grin, not really caring if I still had food on my face. Her smile glowed, and her familiar giggle told me thanks.

Elizabeth had locked herself in a world that was safe to her but peculiar to others. But even though it was difficult to reach her, she often chose to show a special kind of love. And this love, when shared, is forever kept in the hearts of those who find it. I am fortunate to be one of them, and I will forever hold on to the love she granted me.

It's been two years since I began those remarkable afternoons with Elizabeth. Looking back at the time we shared, there is nothing I could ever do to repay Elizabeth or her family for the things I've learned. She has helped me realize that the most precious thing in life is to care for special little children like her. She has taught me to search for things that can be seen only with your heart and that no matter how far the distance between two friends, there is always a hidden love that will bring them together.

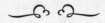

Perhaps kids are so accepting because they see us as we really are as opposed to our temporary poor behavior.

It was the perfect spring day, and we were cruising down Highway 9 in my Jeep on the way to Steamboat Springs, Colorado. A few fluffy clouds on the horizon, a fresh coat of blacktop ahead, and my eight- and ten-year-old daughters playing in the backseat.

Suddenly I got caught behind a very slow-moving farm

vehicle. Although I was in a no-passing zone, I knew I could pass safely because I had a clear view of the highway ahead from my high perch. A state trooper thought otherwise. I fumed silently as this matter-of-fact officer showed no interest in my explanation of safety and wrote out a ticket.

Since my daughters were watching all of this very carefully, I knew class was now in session and I was the teacher. I was courteous to the trooper and accepted responsibility for my mistake, but I was also painfully conscious of the not-so-good example I had already set by disobeying the law. The starchy officer finished his work, and we drove on to Steamboat. That was when the real teachers took over—the little girls sitting in back.

Emmy spoke first. "Daddy, that's so rare for you. You never get a ticket." Ali had a big smile on her face. "I always feel safe with you," she said. "You're such a smart driver."

My first reaction to their comments was shock. My second was to wonder if they were talking about me. I had memories of previous traffic tickets when I had had different passengers. Their comments: "You should have known better." "Why weren't you paying attention to the yellow line?" "How many tickets does that make for you?" "Boy, is that going to mess up your insurance rates."

What's going on here? I thought. Are these two girls sincere? I knew I had screwed up. But, of course, they were looking at the bigger picture and could accept me as a good person even when I blow it. They were looking at my strengths instead of my weaknesses.

ince that spring day I've tried to be a more careful driver even when my daughters are not in the backseat. I've also tried a lot harder to look for people's strengths. Thanks to my daughters, I've discovered that focusing on people's positive qualities actually fuels their desire to excel. Most adults have to work hard at this, while children do it naturally. Let's watch them closely. School is open!

Nevertheless, I strongly believe that accepting our children for who they really are does not necessarily mean accepting all their behaviors. Clear guidelines are still extremely important in establishing boundaries of appropriate behavior and family interaction. However, kids also teach us that acceptance means there's usually more than one "correct" way to do things.

No Right Answer to Life
Peggy Ball
Littleton, Colorado

After four years as a criminal prosecutor and another nine years as a civil trial lawyer, I thought I'd heard it all. Then I had twins. One of the joys I rediscovered was the art of eavesdropping. There's a special quality to the relationship between the two of them that is absent when I'm noticeably in the picture.

One night when my boys were three, we were driving in the car. The moon was only about a quarter full, and I heard Tanner, my ever practical problem solver, turn to his brother and say, "We need to think of a theory for why the moon gets broken." Without batting an eye, twin brother Garrett, ever sweet and fanciful, said, "Cookie Monster ate it. It looks like a cookie, and he took a bite."

Unsatisfied with this whimsical answer, Tanner said, "No. Let me think for a while, and I'll come up with something." After concentrating intently for a few moments, he said with great self-satisfaction, "I know. When the moon comes up, it has to come over those trees. I think there was a broken branch that caught the moon and tore it. Or maybe it caught on the corner of that house . . . or maybe it caught on both, and that's why it has two pointy places."

With very little hesitation, Garrett replied, "Naw, I still think Cookie Monster ate it."

Just like their solutions to this knotty problem, their approaches to life could hardly be more different. Where one is fiercely competitive, the other will let his brother win so he won't feel sad. From their dissimilarities, I have learned a deeper level of acceptance for all people. There is no right answer to life.

—☙ ❧—

Children's willing acceptance of others goes well beyond their families and circles of friends. Indeed, it seems to have no boundaries or border lines.

Hola, Hello, Shalom
Donna Clovis
Princeton Junction, New Jersey

On a beautiful spring day when warm winds blow gently through newly born leaves of trees surrounding the playground, I enjoy taking a moment to watch the children play during recess. I teach English as a Second Language to forty-three children in a public elementary school in Princeton, New Jersey. My classes are rather unique in that the students speak twenty-one different languages and are from all over the world.

As I basked in the warmth of the spring sun, I noticed the interactions of many of the children. "Shalom!" a first-grade child said as she grabbed the hand of a child from Croatia.

"I want to help her, too!" a little Serbian girl said, grabbing the child's other hand. "Let's help her play on the slide." Two five-year-olds smiled at me as they passed and said, "Look, this is my new friend." Nearby I heard the chatter and laughter of some children from South Africa, South America, Korea, Russia, and Haiti as they were playing a circle game.

I thought to myself how wonderful it was that children from all over the world were playing together in peace and harmony. They had transcended all language and racial barriers with their love and smiles. Perhaps I had a glimpse of the future.

I see the possibility of world harmony and peace through the interactions of my students on the playground regardless of race, language, or nationality. Through these young ones may we discover the meaning of true love and friendship. *Shalom. Hola. Bonjour. Halo. Jambo. Ohio. Ni how.* Hello.

CHAPTER THIRTEEN
The Gift of Generosity

———— ❦ ————

Two Used Horseshoes
Jan Serafy
Steamboat Springs, Colorado

A beautiful palomino named Taco was one of the most important things in my life for over twenty years. The riding school where I taught in Atlanta had acquired Taco from the local stockyards. The school's owner and I were appalled at how badly this horse was being abused when we saw him trotted out for inspection. He was being cruelly ridden, his bridle cutting horribly into his mouth as his head was jerked around.

I tried to work with him back at the school, but his head was perpetually up, his ears flared back, and he was totally unwilling to accept a bridle or commands. When I put my foot in the stirrup, he would tear off uncontrollably. At first I tried to shovel a bit into his mouth along with a handful of carrots, but his mouth had been ruined. I had to use a hackamore, a bridle without a bit, and teach him to stop when I whistled. I finally got his head down and turned him into a jumper.

As a special surprise for me, a junior counselor secretly taught Taco to jump free without a rider. That was a tremendous feat for such an abused animal. Taco was very special.

I taught more than 225 students every week, ages six through sixteen. Some were from fairly affluent families and could easily afford riding lessons, but for many others it meant a sacrifice. In fact, I remember one family that had to sell its piano to pay for classes.

Every Christmas we had a party in the stable, and we always had a Christmas tree for the horses—no lights or bulbs, just sugar lumps, carrots, apples, and other horse goodies brought by the children.

On this particular party day, two hundred children presented me with a wrapped box. the usual blouse or scarf, I thought. When I opened it, I found two old, used, beat-up horseshoes. I was at a loss for words but managed to stammer, "Uh, thanks." At that moment one of my students, Karen, came running around the corner of the barn with Taco, who sported a huge red bow around his neck. All the children started singing, "We wish you a merry Christmas," as they gave me Taco!

Two hundred and twenty-five of my students had chipped in dimes, quarters, and dollars to buy Taco from the stable owner for me! In all my sixty-six years, Taco was the most meaningful gift I'd ever received—straight from 225 hearts. But as much as I loved Taco, the children who gave him to me will remain forever my richest memory.

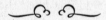

Sometimes the best way to express our love is to give a material gift. But, unfortunately, we often exchange gifts as a matter of routine. The gifts that truly touch us come from the heart. From children, they are extraordinary expressions of love, not obligation.

Think of how much more meaningful and memorable birthdays, Christmases, and all special occasions would be if the gifts we exchanged came from the heart.

I thought the girls' basketball camp started at nine o'clock that Sunday morning. Since it was over an hour's drive from our home, we were up early so we could leave by 7:45. As we finished breakfast, Ali handed me the map and instruction sheet. My glance drifted down to item number three, the camp schedule. "Kids, guess what?" I said. "I just noticed that the camp doesn't start until noon today."

Emmy's reaction was "Great. I can finish my book." Ali's was "Let's go for a walk, Daddy." I smiled at the gift of an unexpected three hours with my daughters.

Walking shoes on, water bottle filled, and Ali and I were out the door. I knew what she wanted to do: Collect wild flowers. I can't swear to it, but I would bet that during Ali's first wobbly steps across the yard at age one, she squealed with delight and picked her first dandelion. From that moment on she gave me endless dandelion bouquets. I shared her delight and excitement with every new arrangement, and her sadness the first time someone told her that a dandelion was a weed.

Ali has always loved picking and arranging flowers—it must be in her genes. About an hour into our walk she was still completely captivated by her work, picking as many different varieties of wild flowers as she could find. Then I noticed something else. Apparently she was allergic to something she had picked and was one continuous sneeze and sniffle.

I mentioned my concern. No response. I mentioned it again. No response again. Had her allergy affected her hearing? Finally, I realized what was going on. Ali was so absorbed in her work and by her desire to create a beautiful bouquet that she didn't even notice her sneezes and sniffles. She simply didn't feel any discomfort because she was so deep into the beauty of giving, caring, and creating.

I remembered the time not long before when the girls' grandmother came to pick them up for a two-week visit with their cousins in Oklahoma. As I watched the big Chevy Suburban pull out onto the main road, I felt the old familiar sadness. I was sure going to miss them. Walking into the kitchen, I noticed the little "baby bouquet" that Ali had surprised me with just as they were loading up. "Here, Daddy," she had said, "this will remind you that I love you." It did more than that. With such a delightful gift, the pain of separation from my daughter wasn't quite so bad.

The Gift of Hello
Lisa Cicchini Bachiller
Arlington, Virginia

Last Saturday my husband and I were enjoying a warm bagel and a fresh cup of coffee at a local cafe. The city was just beginning to awaken to the promise of a rare, perfect, crisp blue autumn day. The car wash across the street already had a line of dusty vehicles running through its whooshing brushes. I could see some drivers sipping coffee while others tried to corral their kids and stop them from bothering the other customers.

Next door, older men sat together talking and reading the paper at a humming fast-food restaurant. I saw a father sharing French toast sticks with his young daughter. Was this his weekend with her? My heart jumped as a picture of my own son flashed through my mind. Suddenly I felt incomplete. Two hours away, my twelve-year-old son was probably just waking up. He'd be hungry the moment his eyes opened. I could see him kicking off the covers, scooping up the cat, and running down the stairs to the kitchen for the first of at least two large bowls of cereal. His dad and stepmom would still be asleep, and my son would eat alone.

I ached for him, longed for him, wished he could be here with my husband and me eating bagels and planning our adventures for the day. A loud, piercing "beep-beep-beep!" pierced my thoughts. My beeper. Hastily I dug through my purse to find the offending little box and shut it off before any more customers looked my way. The message was a long list of 8's: the great Baltimore Oriole Cal Ripkin's number. It was my son's secret code. He had beeped me to say hello.

Instantly, my morning seemed perfect again. My son and I were having breakfast together even if we were physically far apart. He had given me the gift of hello. It was going to be a wonderful day!

Raggedy Angel
Patrick Lee Hawkins
Salida, Colorado

Christmas was a really blue time for me. I was a divorced father who missed the everyday life with my young daughter that I had always taken for granted. I suffered every Christmas until I remembered the Christian adage, "Give to receive." That year I was a DJ at a popular rock-and-roll radio station in Albuquerque and decided to break format (something people can get fired for doing). I told my listeners that I would play requests in exchange for canned goods, clothing, toys, or checks to the Salvation Army.

After I got off the air, I went out to collect those donations. I started feeling a whole lot better knowing that I was helping others rather than feeling sorry for myself. As I was standing in line to check in items at the Salvation Army, I spotted a girl about three years old approaching the counter with her mother. Her little voice rang out in the crowded room as she handed a big burly volunteer the Raggedy Ann doll she had been hugging tightly.

"I've gotten a lot of love from my doll, and I want another little girl to have that love, too," she said.

The devotion that mother had for her daughter radiated from her face, while the smile on the little girl's cherubic face and the sincerity and generosity of her gift warmed my heart. I haven't had a bad Christmas since. Ten years have gone by now, and I've heard that the radio station still makes the annual request for donations. I hope they see that little angel, too!

A Little Birthday Music
Jan Madsen
Lincoln, Nebraska

As I've gotten older, my own birthdays don't hold much magic for me, although they are still special to the children. My thirty-eighth birthday was no exception: The kids were more excited than I was. The day was busy from 6:30 A.M. to 10:00 P.M., and my kids were concerned that they had not been able to go shopping for my birthday celebration. "It's okay," I said. "Don't worry."

So my birthday came and went almost like any other day. The following morning I was busy at work when I heard my phone ringing. I wasn't able to grab it before my answering machine picked up. When I played back the message, I heard a beautiful orchestra playing "Happy Birthday," complete with cymbals. At first I wondered, "Who has this record that they're playing for me?" Then I recognized my daughter's voice among a lot of other voices joining in to sing "Happy Birthday." My daughter's seventh-grade orchestra was playing "Happy Birthday" for me! The message ended with "Happy Birthday! Bye!"

I picked up my daughter from school later that afternoon, and a big smile broke across her face when our eyes met. She couldn't wait to hear my reaction to her birthday surprise and fill me in on the details of her gift. She had had the idea the day before my birthday and cleared it with her teacher. He, too, had thought it was a great idea.

My daughter had planned to make the call on my birthday, but they were not able to get a free line from their music room during orchestra rehearsal. She was disappointed, but her teacher had assured her they could call the next morning. The anticipation made the surprise extra special for her. I still get teary-eyed every time I think about that gift, partly because I'm so proud of my daughter's creativity and partly because she gave me the best gift she could—her love.

A Portrait of Love
Gail S. Ravitts
Rockford, Illinois

The war year of 1944 was tumultuous. First, there was the tremendous, dramatic effort of D-day and then the agonizing disappointment of the Battle of the Bulge that smashed our hopes of peace by Christmas. My personal life was also in turmoil. I turned nineteen in March 1944, and by that time I had soaked many a pillow in loneliness for the young man I had fallen in love with in college and who was then in training to be a navigator in the Army Air Corps.

He graduated in June and received his wings. He came home on leave, and we had two glorious weeks together. He gave me his wings, and I gave him a glamorous studio photograph of myself.

In early September he was sent to Lecce, Italy, as the navigator in the crew of a B-24 Liberator bomber. On October 14, on his eighth mission, he volunteered to take the place of the navigator in a different crew and was shot down over Maribor, Yugoslavia. Some of the men on that plane bailed out and were saved, but he was listed as missing in action and after six months was declared dead. He would have been twenty years old in December. Ironically, the other men in his regular crew all survived the war.

In March 1945 I received an oil painting of myself, done in Italy from the photograph my sweetheart had carried with him to war. He had ordered the portrait, but it was not yet finished when he was shot down. The members of his original crew paid for it to be completed and sent it to me. Shortly afterward, on Easter 1945, I visited my sweetheart's parents and, at his mother's request, left the portrait with them "for a while."

Young hearts can mend, I found, and about a year later I married a fine young man. We had four children. Memories of the portrait and the fallen navigator were suppressed. His mother never contacted me, except once in 1949 to tell me his remains had been returned and there would be a memorial service, which I was unable to attend. I felt a certain estrangement from her, as if she blamed me for his death in some way or perhaps thought I shouldn't have married.

More than thirty years had gone by when our youngest daughter, Tammy, came home for the summer from the University of Chicago with a broken heart. Trying to give her some hope that hearts could mend, that she would find someone else to love, I told her about my early, tragic romance and how her father had been able to fill the empty place in my heart. I also told her about the portrait and that someday I would like to retrieve it from my sweetheart's mother. "As long as it gives her any comfort, I am happy for her to have it," I said, "but she is getting quite elderly, and I'm afraid it might be thrown in the trash at her death."

"Where does she live? Why don't you ask her for it?" Tammy asked.

"Funny," I said, "I even remember her address—113 East Van Buren Street in Naperville. But I hesitate to ask her for it because she has made it quite clear that she doesn't want to hear from me."

When the next Christmas came, it was a time of some financial strain in our family. Presents were pretty small and practical, but we were all grown-ups and we had been through tough times before. Those tough times had perhaps helped give our children the strength of character and compassion for others that some overindulged youngsters might never have. Just having those four wonderful kids all at home for a few days was enough to make the holiday joyous.

My present from Tammy was large, flat, and rectangular. I couldn't imagine what it might be. She certainly had no money to spend, but still it must be something very special, I decided, judging by her smug smile as I tore at the paper.

It was my portrait. I was dumbfounded, absolutely speechless and incredulous. It was more than just my portrait, it was Tammy saying, "Thanks, Mom, for understanding the power of young love and the pain of losing it." It was Tammy saying, "I understand that you were young once, too, Mom." It was one of the greatest gifts I ever received.

A New Access to Life
Amy Jaffe Barzach
West Hartford, Connecticut

Jonathan taught us about joy and the celebration of life. He taught me personally about the importance of enjoying each and every moment, and the virtue of always dreaming, even in the face of tragedy. You can't choose the cards that life will deal, but you can choose to live your life from a positive perspective—no matter what. It is not that choosing to focus on the positive will eliminate the challenges of day-to-day life or completely take the pain of serious illness or death away. But it can help you find a measure of comfort when faced with difficulties, make the best of all situations, and find some meaning in everything.

Wise beyond his years, my son Jonathan was born on April 1, 1994, with a smile and a twinkle in his very beautiful eyes. I've seen many babies, but very few are able to communicate with their eyes like Jonathan did from the very beginning. My friend Diane Samuels once said that he had the eyes of a wise old soul.

During that summer we spent many afternoons at Fernridge Park. One day I was saddened to see a little girl with beautiful long hair in a wheelchair watching from the sidewalk while the other children frolicked on the play structure. Her chin quivered, but she tried to pretend she was just fine. As I held four-month-old Jonathan in my arms and watched my older son Daniel playing—so big, strong, and healthy—my heart broke for this little girl.

Shortly thereafter we discovered that something was desperately wrong with Jonathan. In the fall he was placed in the pediatric intensive care unit of the University of Connecticut Medical Center, diagnosed with an as yet undetermined type of spinal muscular atrophy (SMA). It was then that we remembered the brave little girl from the park.

It soon became clear that Jonathan had SMA type one, a terminal illness that typically causes death before one year. A hospice counselor encouraged us to celebrate every moment we had with Jonathan and to find a way to honor his life—something that would capture his essence. She gently prodded us to think of a memorial that would bring life to the lessons we were learning from him.

It was difficult to think of anything that felt right. At that moment we couldn't even figure out how to save our son's life, and she wanted us to come up with the perfect project, something that would live on after his death. The stress of trying to find just the right thing was overwhelming. But that amazing hospice counselor gently, determinedly, walked us through the process, and slowly the idea of a wheelchair-friendly playground was born.

Jonathan's Dream began as our vision to create a very accessible playground, a wonderful place where children of all abilities would be able to play together, where children with physical disabilities would not be excluded. What started as our family's attempt to cope with the impending death of our beloved son and brother has grown to become a project that has captured the imagination of hundreds of volunteers, community organizations, local businesses, and national corporations and foundations. It has not only helped us with the pain of losing Jonathan but has also reaffirmed our faith in people.

The day before he died, nine-month-old Jonathan was in his crib looking at us as if he knew all there was to know about the celebration of life. Without moving his head or his body, he gave us a lasting gift, an ear-to-ear grin and an intense look of everlasting love in his beautiful twinkling eyes.

Since Jonathan was always full of joy, we decided that his legacy would be a lesson about celebrating life. Now, whenever we do anything with joy for other people, especially children, we feel as though we are doing it in Jonathan's honor. It gives us comfort to think that his goodness lives on in the positive things that we do.

CHAPTER FOURTEEN

The Gift of Forgiveness

Dear Ali,

I am very very sorry for everything I've done to you this morning. And, I forgive you for everything you've done to me.

If you forgive me, cough three times. If you don't, cough once.

Emily

It takes courage to forgive, and Emmy has taught me that sometimes you have to take the first step. My girls constantly demonstrate that there are going to be flare-ups, resentments, and conflicts in the game of life. But if you deal with them, you can go forward. "Forgive and forget" are key words to live by.

Still, that doesn't mean we should ignore it when someone hurts our feelings. Ignoring or stifling hurt feelings causes them to fester into pain and nastiness, and that makes forgiveness all but impossible.

A Divine Apple
Marie Grant
Jamesburg, New Jersey

Although he was in his teens, the job of delivering groceries for our local food market strained Teddy's capabilities. He would never learn to drive a car, so his deliveries were made on an ancient bicycle. I had always had a good relationship with Teddy. I liked him and admired his dedication to his part-time work. I had begun to look forward to seeing him at my back door a few times a week. It wasn't until a day when the heat and humidity had made me testy that I lost patience with the latest of his frequent mistakes.

Teddy, once again, had mixed up my grocery order with a neighbor's. After almost ten minutes of trying to untangle the orders, I lost my patience and screamed at him. I will never forget the hurt, stricken look on the young man's face when he heard my uncharacteristic outburst. After he left, it didn't take long for me to cool down and for the guilt to set in.

I spent a restless night and arose early the next morning to go to the market to find Teddy before he started on his rounds. I found him at the back of the store where he was unpacking a crate of apples. I blurted out my apology and asked him to forgive me for my behavior of the day before.

"I don't know what I'm supposed to forgive you for, Mrs. Grant." Teddy took an apple from the crate and began to polish it on his jacket sleeve. "I don't remember nothin' bad you ever done." He handed me the apple.

Teddy, I thought, how did you become so wise? This is how we should all forgive—by forgetting. I turned quickly to hide my tears. "Thank you for the gift, Teddy," I called to him as I hurried toward the door.

"That ain't no gift," Teddy said with a laugh. "That's just an old apple."

Teddy will never know the value of the gift he gave me that

day. To be forgiving is a humane gesture, but to forget another's sin borders on the divine.

When someone does or says something harmful to us, the temptation is always to strike back and "get even," which makes matters worse. Emmy taught me that there's another—and better—way to react.

I was visiting Emmy's school last winter, meeting her teachers and friends, observing her classroom and admiring her portfolio of achievements. What a neat kid, I thought to myself as we walked to the cafeteria for lunch. She's hardworking, a good team player, and everyone likes her.

"Who are you?" A whiny voice interrupted my reverie.

"I'm Emmy Vannoy's dad," I replied proudly.

"Oh, you mean Emmy *Annoy's* dad?" he jeered.

Little wise guy, I thought. Too bad Emmy has to put up with this type of kid at her otherwise very nice school. I winced inside at how hurt she must be.

Silence. She just kept filling her tray with lunch.

"Emmy," I said, "what do you think about what that kid just called you?"

"Oh, him?" Her voice was light. "Whatever. Doesn't this dessert look yummy?"

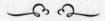

This wise young lady had no need to attack the boy who had insulted her. She was secure in her knowledge of who she was and did not have to defend herself by striking back. If our behavior is based on our own internal values and principles, we don't need to defend ourselves, and we can readily forgive those who hurt us, intentionally or unintentionally. But if our self-esteem depends on the approval of others, we're doomed to be perpetual victims, easily hurt and unable to forgive and forget.

As parents we too often try to teach our children values and principles through guilt, bribes, shame, fear, and control. We trample their spirits, and almost surely the kids brought up that way are going to have an ongoing internal dialogue like this: "I'm not popular. What's wrong with me? I'll never be good enough." Emmy surprised me pleasantly that day because her internal dialogue didn't trample on her own spirit.

Not long ago I heard a mother's fairly typical response to her three-year-old who wanted to stay at McDonald's playland rather than go home. She said, "You can stay, but I have to leave. How are you going to find your way home?" Of course, the kid toddled off right behind her. Her ploy worked, but only because it left the child in total fear.

Another mother nearby was questioning her six-year-old about why he didn't play with his expensive new toy anymore. I couldn't hear his words, but hers rang out clearly. "Well, then, I guess we'll just have to give it away because plenty of other little boys would love to play with it."

Great, I thought. Another child carrying around a load of guilt. I've never yet found that fear or guilt builds any kind of long-lasting, positive internal compass. Kids inevitably make mistakes. That's the way they learn. And we must learn to forgive them. I do not believe, however, that forgiveness means being a doormat. We should never have to condone rotten behavior. The guidelines we use to teach our children principles and values work best when they are jointly defined and lovingly enacted.

Sportsmanlike Conduct
Denis Berkson
Mt. Prospect, Illinois

Michael and I had been invited to a sports birthday party, and I wheeled my seven-year-old son into a gymnasium where a group leader was dividing up sixteen kids for one-on-one soccer or basketball teams. Michael, who is confined to a wheelchair because of cerebral palsy, said, "Dad, I'd sure like to get out of the chair if I could. I don't want to play this in my chair."

"Sure," I said, unstrapping his legs and waist and removing the bar that supports his body. I held him as I usually do under the arms. Braces and all, Michael weighs about fifty pounds, so it's not an easy task to hold him—but it's one I gladly do. I would be Michael's arms and legs as he told me which way to move. When he and I are working together like this, we are bonding in such a special way. He gives himself to me freely, trusting me completely.

Our opponent was a little guy, only about three feet tall, and our job was to kick the ball past him and over the goal line. Then someone would give the ball to the other little kid and let him try to kick it over our line.

We started the game, and I began to run back and forth, holding Michael from the waist, sweat dripping from my face. Michael was screaming with glee. He was so happy that we were doing this. We were running left, running right, going up and down. We almost got the ball over the line.

Michael's legs were flying out in all directions, and I got an image of Alice in Wonderland when she was using a flamingo as a croquet mallet. Then, just as I had Michael's leg swung back to make one final kick, I felt the floor give out from under me. I realized I was falling, falling very fast. I had no way of holding on to Michael, and I looked up to see him flying through the air. Tears filled my eyes before I even hit the floor. Then I heard what sounded like thunder as Michael crashed to the floor.

I was sure I'd killed him. I was sure he was dead. I kept

screaming, "No! No! Please God, please God, let him be all right."

Everyone rushed over to a shrieking Michael. He had had no way to buffer his fall because he had no control over his arms and legs. I felt so bad. I had done something so horrible to my son. I had let his life slip through my fingers. Thank God, he was all right, although badly bruised and shaken. He'd injured his arms and shoulders but had not fallen on his head.

Six days later I was sitting across from Michael at home, just looking at him and wondering if he would ever trust me again. Would he ever let me hold him again, at least in that way?

Suddenly, he looked over at me. "Dad, you know we're kind of lucky, aren't we?"

"Why's that, Mike?" I asked.

"Because," he said happily, "we have sports injuries! Cool, huh?"

Michael, I thought, you are truly a gift. I had your forgiveness. No way were you going to let me impose my own fears and point of view on your indestructible little spirit. And better yet, you've reminded me that trust doesn't disappear because of an unintentional accident or because the situation didn't work out the way you wanted it to. Because you trusted me, you could forgive me.

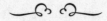

When kids are cranky, grouchy, whiny, or in need of any kind, the best parents, in my opinion, answer that need with love, understanding, and forgiveness. When pain is answered in that way, it heals. I've often seen the same manifestations of children's pain in adults, which comes across as churlishness, selfishness, irritation, and hurt feelings. What would happen if we gave them love, understanding, and forgiveness, too, just as we do a child? Instead, I see us doing just the opposite.

I remember a little girl from my old neighborhood who was always angry at some other child, always resentful. You could see it on her face and hear it in every word she said. There was nothing you could talk about to her since so many subjects were touchy or taboo. Her teachers were mean; nobody liked her; her parents never got her anything she wanted.

This little girl reminded me of the price we have to pay if we cannot forgive and forget. We become resentful, and that resentment lives only in the heart of the person holding it. I've watched that little girl grab her toys away from other kids or refuse to play their games. She stalked off unhappy; they went on playing without her and had a great time.

A Quiet Sign
Sherri Waas Shunfenthal
Burke, Virginia

Some days are too hectic, and there are too many places to go! On this particular day I was tired and cranky because my youngest had kept me awake for several nights with an ear infection, and we had an appointment for a recheck at the doctor's that afternoon. When my two older children came home from school, I shoved a hasty snack at them because we had to get to the doctor's, and they immediately began to complain about being rushed. As we were ready to go out the door, my daughter decided she needed to go to the bathroom, and my youngest son's shoes had come untied—again. My frustration mounted.

Once in the car, the children began fighting. There was a lot of traffic, so I hollered at them that their fighting was distracting me from driving. They were quiet for a brief moment, then started to tease one another loudly. I yelled again that I did not want to hear another sound. There was silence, and I realized that I had screamed pretty loudly myself. But at least it was quiet, I thought.

I figured all three children were sitting in the backseat sulking because I had thundered out my warning. But it sure was quiet back there.

"Mom, look in the backseat!" my daughter suddenly said softly.

"How can I look in the backseat while I'm driving?" I snapped.

"Please, Mom, please," she implored quietly.

"Okay," I agreed. "As soon as we stop at the next red light."

It was quiet for the next few minutes, and I turned around to look when we stopped at a light. All three of my children were sitting quietly with their fingers shaped to say "I love you" in sign language. They started to giggle with the delight of their surprise for me. I almost burst into tears but instead erupted into laughter with them. Here I had been yelling at my children in my frustration with them, but they understood and forgave me by responding to me with love.

Now, whenever I feel like yelling at my children, I think of that special moment in the car. Even in our worst moments, the children respond to me and my husband with love. They have unlocked my own potential for infinite love in responding to the world.

CHAPTER FIFTEEN
The Gift of Encouragement

———— ⌒⟐⌒ ————

A Kiss to Remember
Lisa-Marie Elton
Birmington, Michigan

Being a single parent is never easy. When my son, Shane, was eight weeks old, we left my husband and moved across the country to Michigan where I could be close to my family. I wanted to raise Shane in a more stable, safer environment. I knew that my parents, siblings, and friends would provide emotional support and good influences. I have been fortunate to have such loving support and a happy, affectionate baby. There are times, though, when I forget how blessed I am.

For me, most days are consumed with being a full-time parent and having full-time professional work in and out of the home. Just as you're ending one job, you begin the next. Weekends are just another workday. When bedtime rolls around and the house is again quiet, exhaustion and loneliness set in.

As the stress level rises, my frustration sometimes becomes overwhelming, and I find myself short-tempered. The words "no" and "don't do that" seem to leave my mouth frequently. I begin to question why life is so unfair. I feel as if I am the only one in this situation. I only want to sit and cry while feeling sorry for myself. These are the moments that I forget Shane is just a child, testing and learning boundaries.

Just as I am about to admonish him for the tenth time that day for climbing on the couch with cookies crumbling all over, he puts his arms around my neck, pulls his face close to mine, and holds his lips on my cheek. This kiss always sends tears streaming down my face, which in turn makes him laugh at Mommy crying. Suddenly we are both laughing, and life seems so perfect. I marvel at how a sixteen-month-old can be wiser than his mother.

I realize that life changes daily and children grow very quickly. One day Shane will be a teenager, and then he won't imagine that simply kissing his mother would make her whole world better. But for now, I thank God for an incredible child while I treasure this gift of unconditional love.

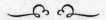

I've discovered that kids have unique ways of giving the gift of encouragement. If I had one-tenth of the belief in myself that Emmy and Ali have in me, I could move mountains.

Emmy and I had four delightful days to explore Boulder, Colorado, while Ali was attending basketball camp at the university. This was a special opportunity because we love to spend time together and because Boulder is a great place to have "adventures." Our favorite spot was the Pearl Street Mall, the restored downtown area packed full of one-of-a-kind art and craft stores, boutiques full of gadgets, ice-cream parlors, and cozy cafes. Emmy was especially fascinated by the '60s-style hippie shops.

The mall also had another feature that captivated us: street performers. There were saxophone, accordion, guitar, and mandolin players, dancers, magicians, balloon artists, and portrait painters in every possible size, shape, and style.

Some had dreadlocks down to their waists, others wore perpetual faraway smiles, and all had colorful costumes and accents from every part of the world. Their instrument cases and jars were always open, and Emmy and I got as much pleasure from tipping the artists as we did buying knick-knacks and ice cream.

When we picked up Ali after her camp each day, we talked nonstop for the first ten minutes, Ali about the camp and Emmy and I about our adventures. Then on the fourth day we decided to take Ali on our personalized "best of Boulder" tour—straight to the mall. She was especially fascinated with one store that had dozens of homemade puzzles. As she sat down to explore, I gravitated to the bench outside the door, nursing a headache. Emmy asked if playing my mandolin might relax me and help my headache go away. Though I realized it probably would help, I said yes reluctantly, because I had never played my mandolin where people consider tipping. My usual playing spots were taxicabs, airport terminal gates, the back corner of an ice-cream store, and on my deck with the case always closed. Also, the performers on the mall were exceptional, and I was only in my second year of lessons.

I got out my mandolin, and just like the street musicians, I was soon lost in my music, very focused and deeply relaxed. Emmy was right: I started to feel better. After two or three songs, she made an unusual request. "Daddy, can I see your case?"

While I continued to play, she opened the case, and a minute later, with a sly, playful grin on her face, she slowly turned it around so the open side was now facing the people who were walking by. Seeing that her strategy had worked so far and that I was going to continue playing, she now requested a couple of her favorite songs and strolled off to a prime observation spot about ten feet away.

Emmy's eyes locked onto every passing face. If they glanced at me, she would perk up. If they smiled at me, she would smile, too. And if they slowed down, she would get downright excited. But no one stopped. After many songs, Emmy's attention and hope had not wavered. Mine had. My heart was breaking. She wanted someone to tip me so very much.

Slowly I began to see things from a different perspective. Just ten feet away from me was a little girl who believed in me with all her heart. I'd seen that same look of unbridled pride, admiration, and faith before. That was all the encouragement I needed. No one had to put money in my case.

Emmy finally went into the store to get her sister, just as a friendly-looking young man approached, stopped, and listened to me play. Then he reached into his pocket and dropped two dollar bills into my case. I had my first tip.

When Emmy returned, she saw the money in my case and expressed her disappointment that she hadn't seen who had tipped me. "Sweetie, a nice young man gave that money," I told her. "But it wouldn't be there without your belief in me. I can't tell you how much it means to me that you believe in me so much. I love you." Her disappointment melted into a beautiful smile.

"Oh, and by the way," I added, "since that two dollars is in there because of you, I would appreciate it if you would use it to buy something special for yourself." She quickly led us to her favorite ice-cream store for a treat.

Still Got Five
Sheri Krug
Parker, Colorado

There's never enough money! That was the mode I was operating in the night I realized we were out of milk—again. My nine-year-old son, Russell, loved cereal for breakfast, and milk seemed to be one of those staples that (1) we couldn't do without, and (2) we always ran out of. I had exactly $3 in my purse. Not enough to buy the special two gallons for $4 deal, but I thought it would cover one gallon and get us through until payday.

Russell said he would run into the store for the milk if I drove him there. On the way he asked if he could get a pop, too. The fear of never having enough money was greater than the guilt of not letting him have a treat, so I said no immediately and told him he had to bring me all the change. He wasn't very happy but didn't dwell on it and ran into the store.

While he was gone, my guilt got a lot stronger, and I was admonishing myself for not letting him get the pop. When he came out of the store and got into the car, he said with a little smile, "I got a pop." With my focus still on the money, I didn't reply and just held out my hand for the change.

He handed me one nickel, then said, "No, I didn't really. I was just kidding!" Trying not to dwell on the fact that almost all of my $3 was gone and wondering why he wasn't more disappointed, I said to him, "You barely had enough money for the milk."

For which I received his wise, loving, and profoundly encouraging reply: "Gosh, Mom, you still have a whole nickel!"

Up in Smoke
Carolyn Gray
Monroe, Louisiana

When my daughter Aimee was five years old, she was beginning to learn about death and losing people you love. Both of my parents had recently died of cancer just two months apart. Aimee and her older sister Tiffany were very concerned about me because I was a smoker, as my father had been. My girls didn't want to lose anyone else they loved and pleaded with me to quit, but I just couldn't seem to find a way.

The next year I was expecting a baby, and Aimee had started a new school year. She had just lost one of her baby teeth and was really excited to find $1.50 that the tooth fairy left under her pillow. She went to her dad and asked how many teeth she had and how much money she would have if she lost the rest of her baby teeth. He figured about $30. Then she asked if she could pull out all her teeth and sell them to the tooth fairy. She wanted, she said, to use the money to help me quit smoking.

When my husband told me what she had said, I wanted to cry. I had never realized what a burden I had put on my wonderful little girl, this child who would do anything for me. Most parents, myself included, make it a point to let their children know how much they sacrifice for them. I can honestly say that I know what it feels like to have my child willing to sacrifice for me.

My husband kept reminding me of what Aimee had said, and I kept trying to quit. I am proud to say that I eventually did, but I don't think I could have done it without Aimee's encouragement. It also warmed my heart every time I saw her beautiful smile, teeth intact. Aimee is now twelve years old, and anytime I get upset with her, her father whispers, "That's your baby who wanted to sell her teeth for you."

Parenting 101
Kathy Post
Denver, Colorado

Over the two decades I have been a parent, I have learned dozens of parenting and life lessons from my daughter, Whitney. I loved her deeply, but after she went off to college and began living on her own in an apartment, our relationship evolved into one that more closely resembled good friends than mother and daughter.

With Whitney out of the house I had more time to pursue my own interests. I was feeling blue one summer, however, because of a combination of professional disappointments: trouble getting a book published, my job not expanding in a way I had hoped, freelance offers of employment not coming in. And perhaps worst of all, I was regretful about missed opportunities in the past. In short, I was suffering from a case of midlife angst that could have been summed up in one question: With all I could have accomplished, what did I have to show for myself?

One day during this time I was visiting Whitney at her apartment and noticed one of her school papers on the floor. I picked it up and studied it for a moment, then asked Whitney if I could read it. It was an assignment she'd prepared for a Parenting 101 class in which students were asked to remember and note ten instances from their childhood when their parents had displayed a lack of parenting skills. After citing each offensive incident, they were to write about how the parent's behavior had made them feel. Naturally, I was extremely interested in Whitney's remarks.

Her first three examples recalled situations I remembered. None of them seemed to be very terrible; for instance, she remembered how angry she had been that she was the only one in her group who had a curfew in high school.

As I continued reading her paper, however, I became more and more confused. In fact, I wondered if my memory was failing me altogether because I couldn't recall anything about my other supposed mistakes. It wasn't until I read her disclaimer at the end of the paper that I understood.

> This paper was interesting to me to do because, although I think I realize how wonderful my mom is, it made me know even more. Over half of these ten "responses" I had to make up because I don't feel negative about what my mom did. I am beginning to appreciate more and more just how lucky I am.

Suddenly, after months of feeling disgruntled about what I had or had not accomplished in my life, I felt happier and more content than I had for years. How shallow I was not to remember what my most important job in life had been! To read my daughter's words was infinitely more satisfying than my job or having a book published.

If ever again I lose perspective on my life's accomplishments, I will go to a quiet place, reread the assignment Whitney wrote, and remember how blessed I have been to have had the "career opportunity" of a lifetime—being a mother to Whitney Post.

Courage, Commitment, Community: A Story in Three Voices
Kevin Tyrell Henry, Hamilton College, Clinton, New York
Thomas G. Smith, Hartford, Connecticut
Vivian Henry, Hartford, Connecticut

Kevin Tyrell Henry: I grew up in Bowles Park, a housing project in Hartford, Connecticut. I don't know my father, and he doesn't matter to me or my life in any way. I never had a male authority figure in my life, although our project had a rec center that was a safe place for kids to go and I could connect with the men who supervised the activities. But I loved my mother most, even though she was an addict. There were weeks and months in my life that she would simply disappear, and I didn't know if she was dead or alive.

My grandmother was a traditional southern woman. She sometimes looked out for me, and when I was with her, there was lots of church and lots of discipline. I respected her and had a good relationship with her and my seven aunts, but I loved my mother and wanted to stick by her. She was so easy to talk to when she was sober. She was beautiful. I loved her so much even though she was doing things I didn't like. Any little attention she gave me, I'd hold on to it until next time. When she was in detox for a couple of months, I knew I had my mom for only that time.

I could always see her potential. I saw her early on as just drugging and not being a good parent. But if her lifestyle hadn't been what it was, I wouldn't be who I am now—independent.

(The following is excerpted from Kevin's application for a Public Housing Authority college scholarship in 1992.)

Working in the community has been a gift that most people take for granted. That gift, unlike being given a new car, is really the gift of having an understanding of life.

First, through service, I have learned to work with children. Second, I have learned to work and counsel people who are addicted to drugs or to any other substance.

Learning to work with children is an important step in life. Growing up in a small community, you tend to understand and recognize what your community is lacking. One problem that I recognized was that there were not enough young, positive role models in my community who the younger children might see. By earning a degree I can show the youth in my community that there is an end to the cycle of poverty.

Every Tuesday and Thursday at the NorthWest Boys Club, I would come in and read a new story to the children; also, I would counsel teens on college and ask them about their future. By establishing a trusting relationship with my community, I think this will make it easier for me to come back and reach out to those who are in need of help. This will be the day when I feel good about myself, because I would know I have made a positive difference in someone's life.

Growing up in a house where your mother is a recovering addict and where most of your family members are using or distributing drugs, you tend to become curious, frustrated, and desperate to make a change. This is what I wanted. I wanted to understand why my mother was using drugs. I wanted to understand where those drugs came from and who made them. All my questions were soon to be answered.

My mother may not have been the best parent that she could have been, but she made sure that all those questions that I had about her addiction were answered. During my mother's recovery, I attended several recovery meetings. I was able to participate and share my feelings and views on the subjects that were being discussed each night. I became heavily involved with the recovering addicts.

I passed out clean needles to the IV users. Also, I gave counseling to teenagers whose parents were recovering addicts, too. I became part of the drug task force in my neighborhood. All this experience helped me understand that people need people and that it does not matter what age you are or what stage of need you are in, the bottom line is that help can be given. The problems that recovering addicts face have an effect on everyone's life, whether it is direct or indirect.

Working in the community has been a gift for me. It gave me a chance to be a part of someone else's life and to have a positive effect on bringing change in the community. Life is all about understanding, caring, and working together. There is no community if people are not willing to work and give their time without expecting something in return. In essence, you always get something in return: knowing that you have made a difference in your community.

Through going to college I hope to come back to my community and give some assistance to those who are going through the horrors I have lived.

Thomas G. Smith, teacher/facilitator, Thomas Snell Weaver High School (excerpts from his recommendation letter for Kevin's scholarship application):

It was probably when [Kevin] said that he would willingly give up playing junior varsity basketball and give up working after school in order to make sure that Jeri, his younger brother, would not have to go home to an empty home, would not have to wait till 6:30 P.M. or so to be able to eat a meal, would not have to be so much of a "latchkey kid" with little adult interaction beyond the close of the school day, would not fall prey to life on the streets, would not be without someone to monitor homework and playtime, would not be without a sense of security and family; it was probably when Kevin gave me this, as his position of logic and thesis, as his statements of conditions, for deciding not to take active participation in a sport so dearly loved. Yes, it was most assuredly at this moment that I realized "Tyrell" was not like most young men in the Weaver High School class of 1993.

I have watched Kevin Tyrell Henry and learned a great deal. I have learned about determination, courage, moral clarity, the essence of spirit, and honest, unrequited love of family and self. I have learned how and when and with whom judgments can, should, and might be in order. I have learned about balance, peace of mind, order, concentration, faith. I have learned about connections that can and should be seen or made between and among things which seem disparate at first but then become wholly related upon deeper reflection.

I have learned that it's truly wonderful to be in awe of things that engender wonderment, to be thankful for things most simple and filled with grace. I have learned that even with people for whom I feel life has been less kind, there is far clearer vision than the vision of people who are without want. I have learned selflessness and how, through giving, there is a spirit of great return. I have learned about "pressing on," about faith.

Kevin has been the model I have watched. No, he does not walk on water but Kevin has changed my life.

Vivian Henry: On a sweltering day in New Orleans, several hundred people honored Kevin Henry at a recognition luncheon for the one student out of hundreds of applicants who had received the Public Housing Authority scholarship. Kevin's long dreadlocks swung against his shoulders as he talked, offering a compelling, emotion-filled speech to an enthralled audience. The master of ceremonies asked if his mother had anything to add. These were her words:

I'm going to die.

You see, I found out in 1988 that I am HIV positive, and I knew I was going to die. That's all I could think about. I was certain my family would no longer want to be around me.

But not Kevin. He went out and did a lot of research. "You don't have AIDS, Mom," he would reassure me. "You're just a carrier. Grab this chance to live."

Eleven years later he still keeps me up to date on medications and treatment. He shows me he still loves me as his mother. He keeps me going.

What he has learned from my addiction, he can use to help other people with their addictions. I can help others, too. We both can use our experience to keep others off the path I followed and he didn't.

I can share my most intimate problems with him—relationships, kids, recovery. Is this my son I'm talking to, I wonder, or is this a friend?

Clearly God put Tyrell in my life when I needed him. I abandoned him, but he never abandoned me. This young man gave me back my life. Who can ask for anything more?

CHAPTER SIXTEEN

The Gift of Love

—◦❦◦—

A Handful of Water
Nancy Calley
Syracuse, New York

Life as I had known it was over. A strokelike condition had robbed me of a rich, full life. My relationships with my husband and children were changed in an instant. As I lay in a hospital bed looking on the wall by my bed at the pictures of my dear ones, a thousand questions flooded my mind. How could they accept a mother and wife who could only be partially there? How would I function with no feeling in my entire right side? I could barely even walk. Why me? It was always someone else who suffered hardships.

I struggled with these and many other questions over the next four years. In the course of my recovery, I was able to walk again and do many of the things I'd thought would be impossible. The time even came that a vacation was again within our grasp. As we packed for our favorite spot in Maine, I realized I still had the ability to dream, an ability I'd thought had disappeared along with my former life. We were eager for the relaxation and healing the ocean would offer. It would be a much needed and well-deserved respite for us all.

I had worked hard to regain as much independence as possible. My family had worked just as hard on goals of their own.

Strength and the courage to forge ahead were apparent in all of us. It would be good to laugh again. And the time spent in Maine was precious. The carefree days and long, quiet evenings were as refreshing as a cool summer rain. But when it was time to head for home, I felt a bittersweet feeling wash over me. We drove slowly while gluttonously drinking in our last ocean view.

Suddenly my husband stopped the car at a very picturesque spot, and without even asking, my family jumped out to absorb one last moment of the ocean's splendor. I swallowed hard to hide a rush of tears when they offered to help me down to the shore. It was my very favorite place on this earth but it seemed a million miles away, so I told them to go on without me.

I sat and tried to enjoy what I possessed—the breeze's gentle dance, the constant rush of the thundering waves, the voices of my children playing, and a dog barking in the background. But a doubting voice came from deep inside me and persisted. Why had God, who had created such beauty and abundance, forgotten me? Wasn't I, too, one of His creations?

As I pondered this, eyes closed, trying to catch hold of some shred of truth, a gentle hand touched my arm. When I opened my eyes, I saw my daughter carefully cupping a handful of water. "If you can't get to the ocean," she said, "the ocean can come to you."

I touched the water in her beautiful hand. Gratefully thanking her, I heard a reassuring voice in the depths of my heart that said, "God remembers us all."

L ove has an amazing ability to nurture and heal. Once again I realize that the wonder of children never ends, nor does the depth of love that shines through all their gifts. Kids seem to know what love is naturally, and their greatest desire is to share it.

After presenting a 10 Greatest Gifts seminar in Greensboro, North Carolina, I was forced to rush a little faster than usual because I was scheduled to arrive at an auditorium in Kansas City by 7:30 the next morning. It would be tight, but my connections through Atlanta should have me at my hotel in Kansas City by 9:30 that night.

At the Atlanta airport I encountered a different problem. Our connecting flight to Kansas City was delayed, once for fifteen minutes and then for another twenty. The crowd at our gate was growing anxious and restless, and I was already worried about getting enough sleep. Then came the announcement that left all of us stunned. "Our flight to Kansas City has been canceled because of unrepairable mechanical difficulties." That was it. No apology. No alternative plan. The loudspeakers were silent.

The noise at our gate rose to an angry roar. Then, just in time, the speakers came alive again. "We are pleased to announce that we have been able to lease an alternative plane, and we will be departing immediately from gate E-46. Please proceed to this gate as quickly as possible."

Groans turned to panic, and our gate emptied in less than sixty seconds. It may have been a sign of my lack of travel experience, but I stayed behind for five more minutes and relaxed with my mandolin. I wasn't terribly excited about being part of this angry crowd, nor was I really pleased about trusting my life to a leased alternative plane.

I blinked hard when I arrived at the new gate. It was in an unused part of the terminal, and it was dark except for a handful of emergency lights. I saw no plane, no airline officials, and more than two hundred passengers who were dangerously close to being completely out of control.

A few minutes later an airline official arrived and

stepped into her worst nightmare. She tried to explain that our plane was being serviced and was expected at the gate within forty minutes, but her words were drowned out by boos, shouts, and angry questions. As the crowd closed in around her, she quickly gave up and had to forcibly push her way through the mob. The last time I saw her, she had lost all appearances of professionalism and was sobbing and running as fast as she could away from the terminal.

For a moment I was fascinated by this seething out-of-control crowd. I actually wondered if someone might have a heart attack or stroke. It seemed as if I was smack in the middle of a vast sea of anger. Then, behind me, I heard some irrepressible laughter. At first I wondered if I was hearing things. This splash of joy was as out of place in this setting as elephants in downtown New York City. I turned around and saw a boy and a girl exchanging delicious giggles and laughter.

The wide-eyed little boy, who must have been about four, ran over to his mother and asked if she wanted to play. His ponytailed sister, probably about seven, was close at his heels. Soon all three were sitting in a circle on the floor playing a game that involved a soft cloth doll and their hands and feet.

Now the magic started to happen. A young couple was watching the fun and asked if they could play, too. Sure! Then a middle-aged woman joined in. An elderly lady asked if she could help keep score. I was so wrapped up in the fun they were having that it took me a moment to realize what had happened. The angry roar had subsided. Most eyes were on the children and their companions, and there were smiles and laughter and conversation almost everywhere.

Those children gave me and many other people a priceless gift that evening. They taught us that life is here right now and not where we are "supposed" to be. They also taught me another life-altering lesson that has been like a shining beacon for me ever since: A sea of fun and laughter ripples out just as fast as a sea of anger. Maybe faster!

And by the way, the plane arrived a few minutes later, and we all made it safely to Kansas City.

A Bunch of Love
Donna Schmidt
Denver, Colorado

I'm on my way to the airport in a total frenzy. The future appears even grimmer. The contracts for this job aren't even complete yet, and the big meeting is tomorrow.

And now, what's that noise? The phone. Here I am trying to navigate my way through rush-hour traffic and avoid the speed traps on the highway to the airport, and someone has the gall to call me on the cell phone. Maybe I'll just ignore the annoying ringing.

No, it could be vital. I'll answer the darn thing.

"Hi, Mommy." It was Liza, my three-and-a-half-year-old.

"Liza, I'm very rushed. I can't talk right now," I snap.

"Mommy, I have to tell you two things."

"Liza, I really can't talk. Bye."

One more time she tries sweetly, "But, Mommy, I have to tell you two things."

"Okay, okay, what are they?"

"Mommy, I love you real hard, and when you get home, I'm going to hug and kiss you a whole bunch," she said.

Suddenly the traffic doesn't matter and the contracts would get done for the meeting. Yes, Liza, I whispered to myself, I love you real hard, too.

I Wish You Loved Daddy
Sue Voltz
Geneseo, Illinois

One day my husband Doug and I got into an argument that ended in heated yelling. I retreated to the porch step and sat with my head in my hands.

Our two-year-old Saralyn had overheard the argument. "I love you, Mom," she said as she came over to sit beside me and put her arms around me.

"I love you, too, Saralyn," I responded.

She rested her head on my shoulder, hugging me hard. "I wish you could love my daddy," she said.

Talk about ripping your heart out! "Saralyn, I do love your daddy. We just had a disagreement."

With that my daughter stood up and walked away. "Where are you going?" I asked her.

"I'm going to tell Daddy you love him."

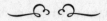

What a sensitive reminder that adults build walls to love; kids walk right through them.

I was having a really rough day. I was grouchy and selfishly thinking of no one but myself while also wondering why everyone was so nasty to me. Emmy and Ali were pulling at my sleeves as we worked our way through grocery shopping, nagging me for pennies to ride the mechanical horse at the front of the store. I gave them a couple of pennies.

The horse was a popular item that day, and the girls had to wait in line. I watched three-year-old Ali wait nearly ten minutes while all the other kids and her sister got their rides. Finally it was her turn. Instead of climbing on the horse, she went over to a little boy who was watching and who she knew didn't have a penny. She put him up on the horse and gave him her ride.

Ali had desperately wanted to ride that horse and had waited patiently for the ride that meant so much to her. Her act of compassion and generosity changed my entire day. "How can I be so selfish and grouchy," I thought, "when that little girl has just epitomized what this world should be like?"

Ali never told a soul what she had done, and she didn't know that I had been watching her. She never knew what a valuable gift she had given me when I saw her stand there with a loving smile on her face as the little boy rode on.

As the Years Melt Away
by Debbie Carey
Savanna, Illinois

The children in my day care center beg me every morning to take them somewhere. Nothing unusual in that, but to a nursing home?

Indeed, that's where they want to go.

Wrinkles, smells, frayed clothes, vacant stares, disconnected conversational fragments, winces of pain—all go unnoticed as the four-year-olds merrily push wheelchairs up and down the hall. As two-year-olds play with colorful afghans and crocheted knickknacks. As infants trace wrinkled faces with chubby little fingers. And especially—oh, most especially—as an old, old woman cries with joy as my infant is placed in her arthritic arms.

Surely no medicine will ever be as effective in melting away the years as the love and warmth and connectedness between young children and these mostly forgotten older people.

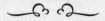

I magine a world in which we all loved others without discrimination, the way children do.

Fathers and Fishing and Football
Randolph Garwood
Texas City, Texas

On that September day I awoke to find the morning air a little cooler, which made me feel alive again after so many hot, humid summer mornings. Living along the Texas coast for most of my life I knew the cooler weather would soon bring some great fishing. My fishing license had expired the month before, so I decided that this would be a good time to renew it and replenish my tackle box, spending the money I'd been setting aside for just those purposes.

My eleven-year-old son asked if he could come with me to the sporting goods store. I went straight to the fishing gear, and he headed straight to the department where the football equipment was displayed. I was looking at a new fishing lure I was interested in when he came up to me with a big grin on his face and a gleam in his eyes. He was carrying a football with his favorite player's name on it, and he begged me to buy it for him.

"I have only enough money for my license and not for both the ball and the license," I told him.

"I understand, Dad," he said quietly, lowering his head as he walked away.

I knew he understood, and being the kid he was, I knew he would never bring up the subject again. But I also realized how important the ball was to him. "Son, if you want that ball, I'll buy it for you," I said.

"But, Dad," he replied, "what about your license?"

"It may be a little early to think about fishing," I said, putting my hand on his shoulder as we walked toward the front of the store. "It might be a few more weeks before it really gets good. And that will give me time to save up for my license. After all, football season has already started."

When we got home, my son headed straight for his friends to show off his new ball. I sat on the front porch with a fresh cup of coffee and watched the boys play. Soon they were resting on the curb right under where I was sitting.

I don't think they knew I could hear their conversation. The subject was football, scores, teams, players. But suddenly I heard my son say, "My dad's the greatest. He gave up something that was important to him just so I could have this football. I'll never forget this day as long as I live. I'll remember what my dad did forever."

Those few words "remember what my dad did forever" sent a chill along my spine while tears of both joy and sorrow filled my eyes. They reminded me of my dad who had died some years before of cancer, which was not a quick and merciful way to die. For two years he suffered with pain and dwindled away to nothing while the family tried to make him comfortable. It was hard seeing a strong man go that way.

For a long time it seemed the only way I could remember my dad was the way he was the last two years of his life. I had forgotten the good memories—the fishing and hunting trips as well as the ball games we used to enjoy together and the sacrifices he made for me that as a young boy I swore never to forget. Why, as adults, do we lose those memories, forgetting the love that was given to us as children?

That afternoon I went to my father's grave site to talk to someone I hadn't really talked to in years. I promised myself from that moment on I would push the sad memories of my father's last days from my mind forever and replace them with all the good memories of my childhood—and all because of those few words I had overheard my son say. He had given me something I will never be able to thank him for, and if I did, he wouldn't really understand, not yet anyway. My son gave me back the real feelings I have for my father and the lost memories. He gave me back the father I knew and loved.

I have finally realized love is so powerful that we don't even have to be in the person's presence to benefit from it. We can express love through prayers or holding someone in our thoughts. Look at the happiest people around you. No doubt they've learned the secret that when you give love, it comes back at least tenfold.

Together Forever
Katanya Berndt
Dublin, Ohio

Some of my best memories are the times when my young daughter would climb into bed with me to snuggle while the sun yawned its way into the morning sky. When she was three, she thought of each new day as a sweet surprise. She chatted on and on about anything that entered her mind while I was only expected to listen as I eased slowly into my awakening.

Eleven years later I can recall only how cold her bare feet were as they pushed against me and how she always smelled faintly of cinnamon. Of all the words she shared with me, I can remember with clarity only the morning she told me that the two of us could always be together.

I thought that statement deserved some response, and I explained to her that one day when she was a grown-up, she might want to live somewhere else. But even if she lived far away, I assured her, we could still talk on the telephone, write letters, and visit sometimes.

She politely let me finish before saying, "No, Mom. That's not what I mean. I mean if you think about me and I think about you, we can always be together."

I was speechless, and as night turned to dawn, I believed it was true that angels never do fall far from heaven.

I knew my parents loved me dearly, but in my entire life, we had never hugged, never said "I love you" in so many words. Ma implied it by baking two loaves of bread before sunrise, packing my lunch every day, and butchering five chickens on the weekend. She was at home waiting for me every day while Pa spent eighty hours a week in the milo and hay fields. We all went to church together every single Sunday except during wheat harvest. I'm sure they had always given me their unconditional love and support, but no one had ever said so.

A couple of years ago I attended a seminar about how to create more love and intimacy in your life. One of our assignments was to tell someone we loved dearly that we loved him or her. We had to decide whom we were going to tell and when, draw up a contract, and sign it. And on the appointed day our seminar "buddy" would call to make sure we had done it.

It was not hard to decide that my parents were the ones I had to talk to. "But I'm not crazy," I told my buddy. "I'm not going to tell my pa I love him, just Ma." That would be easier, I reasoned, so I would start with her and do it over the phone, separated by five hundred miles.

I had never called my parents more than once a week in my whole life, and here it was 11:30 on the Saturday night I'd promised to call. The phone shrilled, and my buddy's voice was insistent. "Well, have you told them yet?" he asked. "This is the day you agreed to do it."

I'd already called my parents twice that day but hadn't been able to summon up the courage to say those three simple words. Both times I'd tried. Both times I'd chickened out. Scared out of my wits, fingers trembling, heart beating wildly, I picked up the phone one more time.

I could picture my elderly mother making her way to the phone. "Hello," she said, her voice reflecting her anxiety that something must be wrong if someone was calling that late at night. On my end, I had trouble steadying my voice. The phone nearly slipped out of my sweaty hand. This was definitely the toughest thing I had ever tried to communicate in my life.

"Hello," Ma said again. "Is anyone there?" I had to say something. "I love you, Ma," I finally managed to squeak.

Total silence at her end of the line. Now I was worried. Maybe she'd had a stroke or something. "Ma, are you still there?"

"Son," she replied, her voice breaking, "we don't talk that way in our family." And she quickly hung up.

The next week I received her usual letter, typically about the cows and the crops and the weather. But in it she said something she had never said before. She closed with the words "We love you, son."

Love in Double Measure
Louise Buchanan
Arlington, Virginia

I held my breath every time she went to the clinic. Would she still be in remission? All of us who loved this child so deeply waited in agony for the results of every blood test. We hoped against hope.

Laura Lue was diagnosed with acute leukemia a year ago

when she was eight. After the diagnosis, however, that vicious disease had remained dormant, noninvasive, deceptively silent —a strange "lull" that caused us at times to deny reality. She went to school as usual, maintaining straight A's. She practiced the Suzuki techniques on her violin. She danced like a ballerina in bloom at her ballet class. But no other nine-year-old from her school or ballet class was having to endure bone marrow tests or blood transfusions or biweekly doctor's exams.

Laura Lue was the daughter of my first cousin, and we just happened to live in the same city during her early childhood. Since her father was the pastor at a huge Baptist church, she and her brother had the unenviable distinction of being "the preacher's kids," an "honor" that required a standard of behavior which cramped their free spirits a bit. But with me they could be just kids! We delighted in wading in the duck pond at the zoo or carving pumpkins for Halloween or building Batmobiles or having food fights with gooey cookie dough. Laura Lue and I were "cuddlin' cousins" and bosom buddies.

On Valentine's Day, 1969, I learned an unforgettable lesson about love from Laura Lue. After an exhausting day I came home to find slipped under my door a white envelope, covered with hand-drawn red hearts, on which my name was boldly written. When I opened the envelope, I found two valentines— not one, but two—and on the back of the top one, in Laura Lue's unique handwriting, I read:

TO LOUISE: HAPPY VALENTINE'S DAY!

I'M GIVING YOU TWO BECAUSE I LOVE YOU SO MUCH . . . !

Who but Laura Lue would choose two valentines because one simply was not enough? Who but she would tuck a second valentine into the envelope to show the full measure of her love?

Leukemia claimed her life eleven months later, but that double measure of love has a grip on my heart to this day. Love that powerful never dies. And sometimes when I wonder if the world has lost its heart, and hate and violence seem rampant everywhere, I reach for those two cards that are among my most treasured possessions. They inspire me to keep trying to make this world a better place through kindness and justice and compassion. My model for loving in double measure is a beautiful child who long ago loved me "two valentines' worth."

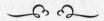

I believe that every child is an opportunity to reconnect with the true nature of love, no matter how long that child may live. Children are naturally the essence and meaning of love. And ultimately they teach us how to be who we really are.

Dottie Jo
by Larry Fortner
Duluth, Minnesota

The woman our son knew as Grandma Fortner (my mother, just for the sake of clarity) was Cleo to her friends.

In her childhood, though, she was Dot.

On some long-ago family trip to visit her dad—eons ago when I was a boy—I heard my Aunt Katie, or maybe it was Uncle George, call my mom "Dot." That struck me as pretty odd, so I asked about it.

My mom was such a little thing when she was a girl, I was told, that everybody called her Dot. She had been so diminutive, just a "dot."

That seemed improbable to me—she was a heck of a lot bigger than I was—but I wrote it off as just another inexplicable thing that grown-ups did.

And now another Dot has come into our lives, and has left.

Our son, Jeff, and his wife, Melody, learned a few months ago that "they were pregnant." (This mutual state of pregnancy still puzzles me, the geezer. I grew up when only the woman was expecting. Now it's some kind of joint project. I haven't figured out the mechanics of this yet.)

The early days of Melody's pregnancy were normal enough, but soon we began hearing distant sounds of alarm. This test seemed a little off. That exam wrinkled the doctor's brow. Something wasn't quite right.

The news grew more troubling with each report and finally took on a grim certainty. Genetic disorders. Birth defects. The child would not survive. Our hearts grew heavy.

Back before the troubles developed, Melody had picked out names for the baby that had family connections. With the coming of the sad news, though, she decided to hold the names for a healthier baby that might come along later.

The little baby she was still carrying, she said, would be Dottie Jo. Melody never knew Jeff's Grandma Fortner.

There is coincidence in this life, and there is coincidence . . .

Dottie Jo was born just before Easter. As babies should be, she was beautiful. And tiny. Just a dot.

She lived long enough to visit with her mother and father and brother and sister and grandmother. She was held and cuddled and loved.

Because of her, our spirits have grown. She awakened little places in our hearts that we didn't even know were there. She touched us with the joy of her presence and the grief of her loss.

Dottie Jo's life ended on the day of her birth. In her time on earth she was pure and entirely innocent. She's the only person we'll ever know whose life was flawless. Perfect.

Planning a burial before someone is even born casts an unreal light on all of life's activities. For several days we were out of synch. But arrangements had to be made.

The little Balsam Township Cemetery in Itasca County, a five-minute walk from the front door of our cabin, has had spots reserved in the name of Fortner for years. In the normal order of life, the old folks would be the first to take up permanent residence in those plots. But our lives had become decidedly not normal. We added more ground in the name of Fortner.

On the cold, blustery Saturday afternoon of Easter weekend, the six of us gathered at the side of the tiny casket in the Balsam Cemetery. We cried more tears. Said our good-byes.

We drove back to the cabin. (I couldn't help but remark that we set the record for being the world's shortest funeral procession: one car.)

We started the sauna fire. Split firewood. Colored Easter eggs. Planned the egg hunt for morning. And Easter dinner. Reveled in the sounds of springtime birdsong. Laughed. Cried.

Life goes on. Life ends. And Dottie Jo has her own little dot of a spot in our hearts forever.*

---

* (Reprinted with permission from *Senior Reporter*, Duluth, Minnesota.)

CHAPTER SEVENTEEN

The Gift of Family and Community

———— ❧ ❧ ————

My life, like so many others, has been transformed by the precious gifts that children offer us every day if only we choose to look, to listen, and to learn from the lessons they teach us.

She loves and she likes and she shares and she shouts and she plays and she cries and, simply, she lives. Why can't we adults be that uninhibited, that content, that simple, that honest?

We don't have to go back to school or to a seminar to learn these lessons. We only have to remember that we already had the magic once ourselves when we were children and were the teachers.

To keep the child happily alive in you and me . . . what greater calling could there be?

Isn't it interesting that when we describe the natural wisdom and magic of children, we are also describing the true nature of love?

Now I hear my daughter say "Hello," and I see what it really means. To the man with the briefcase hurrying by, it says, "A ray of sunshine beams between you and me. All things in it are sparkling and special." To the grocer with bruised bananas it says, "I know your secret desire is to smile at everyone, so start with me." To the woman slumped on the bus stop bench it says, "Your deepest troubles will fall from your hands if you open them to wave at me."

How fascinating the miracles that occur when we see ourselves as our children want us to be.

What a sensitive reminder that adults build walls to love, and kids walk right through them.

Or when we see our children through new eyes.

Be a friend without judging or manipulating or trying to improve someone. Be an ant and someone will bloom.

How much self-pity could we eradicate if only we listened to the real meaning of our children's messages?

A kid doesn't try to keep up with the Joneses. Indeed, his plan of action seems to say, Life is too exciting, exploring the earth too wondrous, to allow other people to live my life for me.

How much more learning could go on if children didn't feel compelled to give us these painful messages:

I don't know what to tell you. If I lie, I'll get in trouble, and if I tell the truth, I'll get in trouble.

And

Naw. No one cares anyway. Grown-ups just tell you stuff.

And how much better we would be if we acted upon their wisdom.

Make sure the students can tell that you really like them, that you care!

Or the wisdom of young Chris, whose mother told me the following story.

It's Time for Love

Chris was jealous of his little sister Lucy from the day she was born. In fact, his jealousy started before she was born. He not only refused to help prepare the nursery and talk about potential baby names, he also refused to come to the hospital. Thank goodness my parents lived close by and we had plenty of baby-sitting help.

We brought Lucy home and of course took lots of baby pictures. It broke my heart when six-year-old Chris scribbled all over every picture. It was even more painful when he refused to hold his baby sister.

We had dreamed of the very opposite: loving siblings and a proud big brother helping his little sister learn about life. But it wasn't to be. In fact, the worst was yet to come. For the first six months of Lucy's life, she could barely cry without Chris screaming for attention. And at the age of three or four, when Lucy would beg her brother to play with her, he would call her a stupid baby and walk away.

Our pediatrician, Dr. Ippen, said that Chris's reaction was exaggerated but normal, and it would eventually pass. I had my doubts. It seemed to us that the more Lucy loved her brother, the more he rejected her.

The saddest moment for me was right before Lucy's sixth

birthday. She had invited eight children to help her celebrate, but her most important guest would be her brother, Chris. A full month before her party, Lucy spent the entire afternoon creating a special invitation for her brother. When she gave it to him, Chris simply wadded it up and walked away, saying, "I'm not going to her baby party."

On the day of Lucy's party I noticed him stop by the door to the dining room and look longingly at the partygoers. I had also found Lucy's birthday invitation smoothed out and tucked under some books on his desk. Later that evening I couldn't hide my pain and tears when I heard Lucy explaining to her friend Susan that her brother didn't love her. Yet maybe, just maybe, he did.

Two months after her sixth birthday, we took Lucy to Dr. Ippen because she had experienced several days of an increasingly painful headache. A 6 A.M. hospital check-in the next day for further testing was evidence of the doctor's concern. Three days later we had to face our deepest fears. Lucy was diagnosed with a rare, terminal disease, and she was given only two to three months to live.

It was funny, but I think I was more worried about Chris than any of us. I didn't know how to tell him and had no idea how he would react. And to make matters worse, it seemed as if he even resented her illness. It must have seemed like just one more way that she would get all of the attention.

Less than two weeks after Lucy was diagnosed, I went upstairs to give her an early-morning medication. I couldn't wake her and was afraid she had slipped into a coma. In a panic I ran downstairs and called Dr. Ippen, who was also an old family friend and lived in our neighborhood. He was at our front door in less than five minutes and took the stairs two at a time. I just stood there in a paralyzed state, hanging on to the banister and looking up at the doorway he had just entered.

His face said it all when he came out of Lucy's room a few minutes later. My little girl wasn't going to wake up. The next thing I remember was my husband trying to comfort me later that night. He said I had wavered between crying and screaming the entire day.

In my agony I had forgotten completely about Chris. My husband said he was in his room and that he had already told him about Lucy. I ran to Chris's room and burst in to hold and comfort him. But while I sat on the edge of his bed sobbing my eyes out, Chris just patted me on the shoulder and said it would be okay. He never shed a tear.

Chris refused to go to his sister's funeral. For another two weeks he refused even to talk about his sister's death and showed no visible sadness or emotion of any kind. Then about three weeks after we lost Lucy, Chris invited his friend Shawn over to play Nintendo. Good, I thought, at least he's starting to spend time with his friends again. Later that afternoon when I was coming down the stairs, I overheard Chris at the front door with his friends. His words stopped me in midstep.

"Listen Shawn," he said, "there's one thing you've always got to do. Every single night, tuck your little sister in bed and tell her you love her."

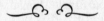

How important it is to treasure our children and their many gifts. And if childhood is a classroom, how important it is to learn the lessons that our children teach. They demonstrate daily what life and family and community are truly about.

It seems very clear that many of our current models of family and community don't work. How else to explain the daily litany of crime, drugs, abuse, broken families? "Just say no" seems futile advice. Abuse programs aren't stopping abuse. Cops aren't stopping crime. All of our complex, technical, expensive solutions are only temporary Band-Aids and in many cases actually perpetuate the problem.

I do not know of any single solution to all that ails us, but something does work that costs nothing. What if we could start to build community together as defined by Kevin, one of those kids whose circumstances might have doomed him to the growing list of victims of drugs and crime?

> Working in the community has been a gift for me. It gave me a chance to be a part of someone else's life and to have a positive effect on bringing change in the community. Life is all about understanding, caring, and working together. There is no community if people are not willing to work and give their time without expecting something in return: In essence, you always get something in return: knowing that you have made a difference in your community.

You can. We can. Our children are already showing us the way.

Through these young ones may we emulate the meaning of true love and friendship.

Shalom. Hola. Bonjour. Halo. Jambo. Ohio. Ni how. Hello.

THE 10 GREATEST GIFTS PROJECT

We all have outstanding dreams and visions about what our lives will be like when our children are born or adopted or blended into our families. But all too quickly the demands of modern life begin to chip away at our vision with the perpetual demands and problems of schedules, jobs, finances, and the endless to-do lists of daily activity.

Parents and educators who have attended our sessions say, "This has turned our family/classroom from crisis to joy." "This has brought me back to the joy of parenting." "I just never realized how proactive I could be in giving my children and students the really important things—the qualities and values that develop internal commitment and responsibility."

The 10 Greatest Gifts Project provides keynote addresses, workshops, seminars, articles, research, organizational assistance, and newsletters dedicated to helping families, schools, and organizations get back in touch with their dreams and visions—and how to achieve them. For more information regarding the 10 Greatest Gifts Project facilitator certification, or for information about audio and video tapes or other materials, please call 800-569-1877 or write to The 10 Greatest Gifts Project, P.O. Box 5301, Denver, CO 80217.

From all of us at the 10 Greatest Gifts Project,
thanks for caring enough to give the gifts
of internal qualities and values to your children, students,
grandchildren, and all the children of the world.